# the
# year
# of
# less

*"If you've ever felt there must be more to life than consumerism and its vicious cycle, you'll find inspiration to break free in* The Year of Less. *Cait's highly readable and personal story is encouraging, challenging, and unbelievably helpful."*

— **Joshua Becker**, author of *The More of Less*

*"Cait Flanders is a brave woman. As I read, I cried. But my heart also brimmed with joy. For anyone who doesn't think they can, Cait's story shows that it doesn't matter where you start, only where you go from there."*

— **Gail Vaz-Oxlade**, host of *Til Debt Do Us Part* and author of *Debt-Free Forever*

*"Cait's audacious goal—a yearlong shopping ban—has sparked a deeply personal book full of lessons for all of us on finding more fulfillment and meaning in our lives (without all the stuff!). A game-changing read for anyone searching for simplicity in our consumer-focused world."*

— **Rachel Jonat**, author of *The Joy of Doing Nothing*

*"*The Year of Less *is beautiful, vulnerable, and real. Cait's words inspired me to be braver in my writing and life, and I'm sure it will inspire you too."*

— **Tammy Strobel**, author of *Everyday Adventures Journal* and *You Can Buy Happiness (and It's Cheap)*

*"Minimizing belongings in my life cleared space for so much goodness to fill the space stuff once did. Cait's* The Year of Less *is inspiring . . . a powerful example of how transformative downsizing possessions can be, and how you can take it to the next level."*

— **Katie Dalebout**, author of *Let It Out*

# the year of less

how I stopped shopping, gave away
my belongings and discovered life is worth more
than anything you can buy in a store

## CAIT FLANDERS

**HAY HOUSE**

Carlsbad, California • New York City
London • Sydney • New Delhi

**Published in the United Kingdom by:**
Hay House UK Ltd, Astley House, 33 Notting Hill Gate, London W11 3JQ
Tel: +44 (0)20 3675 2450; Fax: +44 (0)20 3675 2451; www.hayhouse.co.uk

**Published in the United States of America by:**
Hay House Inc., PO Box 5100, Carlsbad, CA 92018-5100
Tel: (1) 760 431 7695 or (800) 654 5126
Fax: (1) 760 431 6948 or (800) 650 5115; www.hayhouse.com

**Published in Australia by:**
Hay House Australia Ltd, 18/36 Ralph St, Alexandria NSW 2015
Tel: (61) 2 9669 4299; Fax: (61) 2 9669 4144; www.hayhouse.com.au

**Published in India by:**
Hay House Publishers India, Muskaan Complex, Plot No.3, B-2,
Vasant Kunj, New Delhi 110 070
Tel: (91) 11 4176 1620; Fax: (91) 11 4176 1630; www.hayhouse.co.in

A catalogue record for this book is available from the British Library.

Tradepaper ISBN: 978-1-7818-0859-7
Hardback ISBN: 978-1-4019-5487-1
E-book ISBN: 978-1-4019-5352-2

Interior design: Joe Bernier
Cover design: Kathleen Lynch

Printed and bound by CPI Group (UK) Ltd, Croydon CR0 4YY

*For my family, and for Molly and Lexie.*
*I'll miss you forever, sweet girls.*

# contents

# introduction

The idea was born on a trail, as many of mine seemed to be. It was two days before my 29th birthday, and my girlfriends and I decided to celebrate with a weekend in Whistler. We were hiking around Cheakamus Lake in Garibaldi Provincial Park, where the shade of the turquoise water changed as often as every new patch of clouds rolled by. Our topic of conversation shifted just as quickly, ranging from our work and hobbies to friends and relationships.

Wendy had recently moved in with her longtime boyfriend, and Liz was getting ready to do the same with hers. They were both talking about what was next: buying houses before prices in our hometown of Victoria, British Columbia, got out of control, and considering having kids before getting married. After working as the managing editor at a financial startup for two years, I shared what insight I had, but felt that was all I could contribute. While my friends were moving on to the next stages of their lives, I was still working on myself.

"What's next for *you*, Cait?" Liz asked. It was a simple enough question from one of my oldest friends. Liz and I had first met in eighth grade. We only went to the same school for a year, but a year was all we needed. She lived down the street, and we could often be found walking between our two houses to hang out at one or the other. After all these years, I imagined she might have been hoping I would say I was finally ready to settle down too.

Knowing me, though, she probably *expected* me to say I was going back to Toronto for work soon or moving to yet another new city. I was always on the move.

Instead, I shared a thought I'd been sitting on all week.

"I've been thinking about doing an experiment where I don't shop for a while," I replied. "Like, maybe six months or even a year."

My friends were no longer surprised when I made announcements like this. In the previous three years, I had made many big changes in my life, including committing to getting (and staying) out of debt, taking control of my health, and quitting drinking. I had also publicly documented these changes on my blog (caitflanders.com, formerly known as "Blonde on a Budget"), which I started writing in 2010. After the words "Cool!" and "That'll be interesting!" came out of their mouths, they rushed me with a list of follow-up questions. Now that I had said the words out loud, I felt the intention take hold and the plan begin to form. We talked about what the experiment might look like, including what I would and wouldn't be allowed to shop for.

I didn't have all the answers yet. I never had all the answers, when I started one of my experiments. The same way I didn't know I would be capable of paying off $30,000 of debt in two years or losing 30 pounds in one year, I had no idea that during the next 12 months I would end up living on 51 percent of my income, saving 31 percent, and traveling with the rest. I also didn't know I would document so much of it on my blog, or that the stories and lessons I didn't share online would eventually become this book. All I knew was I still wasn't happy with my financial situation, and I wanted to start spending less and saving more money. That's where this story begins. That's where *most* of my stories begin.

When I was nine years old, my parents took me to the bank where, together, we opened a children's savings account. It came with a small booklet to record my deposits and the subsequent balance of my account. The booklet contained no more than 10 pages held together with two staples, but it had my name on it and I treasured it. Writing numbers in it made me feel like I was a grown-up—responsible for something bigger than my toys. It lived in my desk drawer, sandwiched between my elementary school planner filled with homework assignments and my diary. That's the first memory I have of my parents talking to me about the importance of saving money. Unfortunately, the novelty quickly wore off, and I lost the booklet, along with any interest in managing my finances.

As a teenager, I would often come home from school to find my bed littered with newspaper articles. Stories about interest rates, retirement savings plans, real estate markets, and economic forecasts had been cut out and laid flat for me to see. This was always my dad's doing. Every morning, he drank a pot of orange pekoe tea at the kitchen table and read the paper from front to back. If I wasn't sitting next to him, so he could physically put a page in front of me, he would cut it out and place it on my bed. "Did you get a chance to read that article?" he would ask, shortly after I walked in the door from school. "I'll do it *later*," I always whined.

Later didn't come very often and my dad knew it. He would play Twenty Questions about the articles at the dinner table, which often turned into one of his rants that took a simple example and made it extreme. That's usually when he lost me. "This stuff is important, Caitlin!" he would say, at the exact moment my eyes glazed over. I knew he meant business when he called me by my full name. Nobody ever called me Caitlin, unless it was serious or I was in trouble. Still, I stared into the trees of the Emily Carr painting on the wall across from me, nodded my head, and repeated back some of what he had been saying. But I always started with the two words all parents roll their eyes at: "I know." I knew everything back then.

As boring a topic as it seemed at the time, I now realize how lucky I was to grow up in a family that talked about money. Actually, we talked about everything. When your dad is a sailor, no topic is considered taboo. From what you were doing in the bathroom, to the sometimes crude but honest advice about what not to do with boys in the bedroom, we shared all the dirty details with each other—or, at least, my parents thought we did.

For as honest as I was with my family about some things, I also kept a lot of secrets from them. When I was a teenager, my parents thought I saved the allowance I earned for babysitting my younger brother and sister, but I never told them I spent most of it on alcohol and drugs. By the time I finished college and moved out of my parents' house, they had taught me all the basic rules about how to manage my finances, but I never told them I'd been in debt since the day I got my first credit card. My dad got sober when I was 10, and he always knew I drank socially, but I never told him I drank alone or that almost every first sip eventually led to me blacking out. And my family saw me eat well and hike a lot, but I never told them how often I ate chocolate in the car or ordered pizza when I was home alone.

I wasn't just lying to my family about these things—I was lying to myself, mostly about what all of it was doing to my physical and mental health. The higher my credit card balance was directly translated to how little sleep I got at night. The more I drank, the worse I felt about myself. The more I ate, the more weight I gained, which also added to (or rather, subtracted from) how I felt about myself. And the longer I pretended these things weren't happening, the worse it all got.

After months of ignoring my credit card statements, I finally looked at the numbers in May 2011 and realized I was maxed out with nearly $30,000 of consumer debt. To make things worse, I only had $100 left in my checking account and $100 left on one credit card, all of which had to last for six weeks until I would get my next paycheck. At the time, I was also the heaviest I'd ever weighed (209 pounds on my 5'7" frame is considered obese). And, at 25, I had just moved back into my parents' basement after attempting to move across the country for work and drinking away my entire savings in only eight weeks.

The weight of the debt on its own was crushing. I cried myself to sleep for weeks, feeling as though I'd lost my chance of having any kind of strong financial future. I also worried I couldn't come back from the disappointment my parents must have felt, and that I'd failed to be the role model my brother and sister needed.

But some of the tears I shed were for the other things I knew I was going to have to change. I'd attempted to quit drinking before, but had never lasted more than a few weeks. And I'd gone up and down on the scale more times than I could remember, but this high number was a new low for me. It turned out I didn't actually know everything. I knew a little, but not enough to prevent me from getting to this place. I had reached my personal rock bottom, and I didn't want to know what I would find if I went any deeper. The "one day" I had always told myself I would turn things around by was finally here.

In the two years that followed, I paid off all my debt, took control of my health, moved to Toronto and then Vancouver, and quit drinking for good (after a few more failed attempts). I documented all the changes I was making on my blog, which brought in more and more readers with each update. I won't pretend any of it was easy, and I can't tell you I followed all the experts' advice. I just did what worked for me, and I was grateful to have people to stay accountable to.

After those two years, I should have been set up to live a much happier and healthier life. I had done the hard work and proved I could tackle anything I set my mind to. Instead, I went right back to some of my old ways.

I didn't start drinking again, but I did start spending almost every extra penny I had. It seemed harmless, at first. Spending an extra $5 here and $10 there. Walking into stores for one or two items and walking out with five. But the dollar amounts climbed quickly as I began justifying the cost of going out for brunch more often and buying new books whenever I wanted them. Eventually, I started traveling home more frequently and, from there, going on more weekend getaways with friends. I won't deny that it felt good. After two years of living on an extremely tight budget, it felt good to have some freedom and flexibility again—to be more spontaneous and able to finally have some fun. What didn't feel good was never being able to reach my savings goals, and then having to explain to readers why I hadn't.

When I was paying down my debt, I had a practice of sharing my tentative budget at the beginning of each month and posting the final numbers at the end. During those two years, there were months when I put up to 55 percent of my income toward debt repayment. It was a tad aggressive, but I did whatever I had to in order to get my balances down to $0. When that day finally came, I felt freer—lighter—and like the world had opened so many new doors for me. For the first time in my life, I could set real savings goals, like putting aside 20 percent of my income for retirement.

It was doable. It should have been doable. But it was still harder than I expected. For the first year I was supposedly "freer," I continued posting my final numbers at the end of each month, and I was lucky if I could report that I had saved even 10 percent.

I didn't come up with the idea to do a shopping ban, as I called it, overnight. The seed was planted once a month, at the end of every month, for 12 months in a row. Every time I had to write an update and justify why I was barely able to save any money, I told myself I could do better. I could save more, and I knew it. I simply wasn't sure where to begin making changes. It wasn't until the entire Flanders family was sitting around a table, having one of our usual rants about all things money-related, that I finally had my aha moment.

After we'd given my sister, Alli, a hard time for spending hundreds of her hard-earned dollars on something we didn't think she needed, she delivered a rebuttal she had seemingly saved just for me. "I save 20 percent of my income, so I can spend the rest of my money on whatever I want." She was only 20 years old, going to university full time and working part time—and she had figured out the secret before I did. Save first, spend what's left over. Still, as her big sister, I felt the need to dig deeper. "But you live at home. Do you really need 80 percent of your income, or could you live on less?"

As soon as the words came out of my mouth, I realized how hypocritical I sounded. Then the wheels started churning.

That conversation took place one week before my hiking trip in Whistler, and I spent the next seven days looking at my numbers and asking myself some serious questions. *If I was only saving up to 10 percent of my income, where was the rest of my money going? Why was I continually making excuses for my spending? Did I really need 90 percent of my income or could I live on less?* I had been asking myself similar questions at the end of every month for 12 months in a row, and I still didn't know the answers. All I knew was that I seemingly had everything I wanted in my home, in my career, and in my life, and it never felt like enough. I was never satisfied. I always wanted more. But since more of anything wasn't filling me up, maybe it was time to challenge myself to go after less.

When I returned from the weekend in Whistler, I sat down to type up my plans. The rules for the shopping ban seemed simple enough: For the next year, I wouldn't be allowed to buy new clothes, shoes, accessories, books, magazines, electronics, or anything for around the house. I could buy consumables—things like groceries, toiletries, and gas for my car. I could purchase anything I outlined on my "approved shopping list," which was a handful of items I could look into the immediate future and know I would need soon. I could also replace something that broke or wore out if I absolutely had to, but only if I got rid of the original item. And I would still be allowed to go to restaurants on occasion, but I was not allowed to get take-out coffee—my biggest vice and something I was no longer comfortable spending $100 or more on each month.

At the same time I decided I couldn't buy anything new, I also decided to get rid of everything old I didn't use. One glance in any corner of my apartment showed me I had more than I needed, and I didn't appreciate any of it. I wanted to start using what was already in my possession. I wanted to feel like everything had a purpose, and that whatever I brought through my front door in the future would also have a purpose. If I couldn't do that, it had to go.

Before I hit "Publish" on the blog post and announced my plans to readers, I added a line that said, "I've made mindful decisions to get out of debt, stop excusing my laziness, and cut drinking from my list of hobbies. However, I'm still not the mindful consumer I'd like to be." I wanted to stop making impulse purchases only to realize I had been fooled by another marketing strategy or sale sign. I wanted to stop wasting money on things I thought I needed, only to come home and find I already had more than enough. And I really wanted to stop talking myself into buying things I would never end up using.

I wanted to get to a place where I only bought things I needed *when* I needed them. I wanted to finally see where my money was going and budget in a way that aligned with my goals and my values. And I really wanted to start spending less and saving more. But it would never happen if I continued to make mindless spending decisions.

I would start this challenge the next morning: July 7, 2014—my 29th birthday and the beginning of my 30th trip around the sun. And I would go on to share numerous updates on my blog about what I learned during the year of less. It was about the spending, the money. That's where this story begins, and where many of my stories have begun. But there were so many other things I was hesitant to share that year—events that pulled the life I'd known out from under me and left me standing on my own—or rather, left me in bed for weeks, thinking about giving up on all the positive changes I'd made. During what was supposed to be a simpler year where I pursued less, everything I loved and relied on was taken from me, and I was forced to start from scratch and make a new life for myself.

I didn't share those stories on my blog as they were happening. I trust my readers would have supported me, but I was too shattered to piece together the sentences. Every time I tried, I would fall apart and delete the draft post. I couldn't talk about it then, but I want to share it all now—here, in this book, with you. In the chapters ahead, I'll walk you through my year of less as it happened. Along the way, I'll also take you with me through things that happened in the years and decades before. It's only with this information that you can see the full picture and understand why the year of less was so important. It challenged me. It turned my life upside down. And then it saved me.

# Rules for the Yearlong Shopping Ban

What I'm allowed to shop for:

- Groceries and basic kitchen supplies
- Cosmetics and toiletries (only when I run out)
- Cleaning products
- Gifts for others
- Items on the approved shopping list

What I'm NOT allowed to shop for:

- Take-out coffee
- Clothes, shoes, accessories
- Books, magazines, notebooks
- Household items (candles, décor, furniture, etc.)
- Electronics

Approved shopping list:

- One outfit for multiple weddings (one dress and a pair of shoes)
- Sweatshirt (I only owned one and it had a few too many holes)
- Workout pants (I was down to my last pair)
- Boots (I had nothing appropriate for fall/winter)
- Bed (mine was 13 years old and desperately needed to be replaced)
- I can also purchase anything that must be replaced, but the original item has to be tossed or donated

And I must stay accountable on my blog.

# 1

# july: taking inventory

**months sober:** *18*
**income saved:** *20%*
**confidence I can complete this project:** *100%*
*(but I still have no idea what I've signed myself up for)*

I have always been a neat freak. When I was a kid, my parents never had to tell me to clean my bedroom. Everything I owned had a place or drawer or container it belonged in, and it all lined up. The clothes in my closet were hung by article type: tank tops, short-sleeve shirts, and long-sleeve shirts first, then pants, skirts, and dresses at the back. Even the books on my shelves were organized by size and then by the color of their spines.

In elementary school, the inside of my desk looked the same. On the right side, a stack of file folders was arranged by the colors of the rainbow: red on the top, pink on the bottom, with orange, yellow, green, blue, and purple in the middle. On the left side, my pencil case sat on top of my dictionary, which sat on top of my math textbook. Inside that plastic container, I managed to store my erasers in one corner, white-out in another, and kept my extra pens and pencils lined up in a row. I even went so far as to keep all 24 of my pencil crayons in color order in the box.

Whenever teachers gave us time to clean out our desks, I sat still and watched my friends suffer through the ordeal. Crumpled-up notes, used plastic sandwich bags, and lost library books fell to the ground. Loud groans and heavy sighs came from all directions, as my friends took every last item out, then realized they had to find a place for it all. In these moments, I secretly hoped they would ask for my help—and am certain I appeared too eager when they did.

I have maintained this standard of tidiness in every space I've called my own. The lockers I've used, cars I've driven, apartments I've lived in, boxes I've packed and stored, and even the wallets and purses I've carried on a day-to-day basis. If you ever looked inside something I owned, it was organized—until it wasn't.

I started losing things in the spring of 2014. My green tank top was the first item to go missing. It was the only green tank top I owned, and it had always lived on the right-hand side of the second drawer in my three-drawer dresser. One morning, I opened the drawer and was surprised not to see it there. I searched through the stacks of other tank tops and T-shirts that filled the space, then dug through the two other drawers. No green tank top. It wasn't in the closet, or the dirty laundry hamper, or even the washer or dryer. It was simply gone, never to be found, swallowed up by the same monster that always stole my socks.

After that, it seemed like I couldn't find anything when I needed it. The extra tube of toothpaste I could've sworn I had put in the bin of other toiletries under the bathroom sink. The pink bathing suit I didn't even like but had kept because I knew my black one was nearing its final days. And the can opener. I was one person who had one utensil drawer and one can opener inside of it. Why wasn't the can opener inside of it?

While looking for the things I actually needed, all I could see was everything I didn't. The five black tank tops that were too big now that I was 30 pounds lighter. The endless supply of lotion and shower gel I continually added to, without using up what I already had. The summer and winter clothes I rarely wore in Port Moody, B.C.—a city with one of the mildest climates in Canada. So much of it had been purchased with one of two credit cards, back when I was racking up my old debt, but I never used it. Some items still wore their original price tags.

One thing debt and clutter have in common is that as soon as you start letting it pile up, it can be harder and harder to see your way around it. I ignored my debt for months, peeling back only the corner of my credit card statement envelopes to see the minimum payment due. That trick only lasted for so long, until the day came when I saw the total balance and realized it was within $100 of my limit. The math was simple. I had dug myself into a hole too deep, and had no choice but to start clawing my way out of it.

My clutter situation wasn't quite as dramatic. When I walked into my apartment, it looked as put together as always. The towels were all folded, clothes hung in their usual order, and every shoe sat in its pair. Even my books were still organized, only now by genre—fiction, memoirs, business, and personal finance—and then by size (and sometimes still by color). The problem, again, was that I didn't use most of it. And I was reminded of this fact every time I had to walk past it and look at it.

I first thought about this after moving five times in 2013. Each time, I pulled boxes out of one closet, carried them to a truck, drove to my new place, carried them inside, and then placed them in my new closet—all without ever really looking at what they contained. I did this five times, for a number of unfortunate reasons: one time, feeling unsafe after someone tried to break into the only ground-level apartment I've ever lived in while I was home recouping from a car accident; another time, having a longtime friend and brand-new roommate tell me he wanted to relocate to a new city only five days after I moved in with him. It was a tough year.

My last move, in September 2013, had brought me to this apartment in Port Moody. I had only been to the city two times before that, but had quickly fallen in love. It was far enough away from downtown Vancouver that you felt like you were in a small town, and it curved around an inlet so the ocean was always close by. My desk sat in front of floor-to-ceiling windows that overlooked the trees and mountains. Friends often commented that it looked like I was living in a *Twilight* movie, which wasn't far off, since most of those movies were filmed in B.C., including a few scenes in Port Moody itself.

For a full-time editor who worked remotely for a financial startup, this apartment and its views—and my life, to some degree—looked like a dream come true. However, you can only spend so much time working from home before you eventually notice what else is in your surroundings: your stuff. And even though mine was neatly organized, there was still too much of it, and too much that did nothing but collect dust.

I wish I could say the story of why I decided to declutter was more interesting or meaningful or dramatic, but that would be a lie. The truth is, it was a decision made only after thinking *I should get rid of some of this stuff* countless times before. It was the same way I used to think *I should stop using my credit cards*, or *I should stop binging on junk food*, or *I should stop drinking so much*. The excuse I would always tell myself was that I would do it "one day."

One day always did come, eventually. One day in 2011, my credit was maxed out. On the same day in 2011, I was within a few pounds of needing to shop in the plus-size section. One day in 2012, I was unwilling to wake up from another blackout. In all of those instances, I probably could have found ways to carry on with my bad behavior. I could have called the credit card companies and asked for higher limits, or continued eating and drinking too much and ignored what it was doing to my body and spirit. But one day, I knew enough was enough. The stories I'd been telling myself to allow these bad habits to continue for so long had reached their ending. I was done.

And one day in July 2014, I was also done—done with searching through all the things I didn't need to find the one thing I actually did.

Of all the objects that could push me over the edge and inspire me to finally declutter, the can opener is what did me in. I wanted to add some black beans to a salad, but I needed the can opener to make it happen. The only problem was: I couldn't find it. I searched every drawer and cupboard in the kitchen. I searched the sink and the dishwasher. I even looked in the recycling, thinking maybe I accidentally dropped it in there when I threw out the last can I had opened. But it was nowhere to be found.

It was the first week of July and Greater Vancouver was in the middle of a heatwave. Temperatures hovered around 34°C (93°F) and were over 40°C (104°F) with humidity. I lived on the 22nd story of a cement building that didn't have air conditioning, which only made things worse. I was hot. I was hungry. I was frustrated. All I wanted was my stupid black bean salad, but I couldn't have it. Instead, I was stuck with a plain salad and my choice of 21 forks to eat it with.

"One day" had finally come, and I was ready to get rid of everything inside the utensil drawer—and in the rest of my apartment—I didn't need. And much like the days when I decided to start paying down my debt, to eat better, to exercise more, and even to (finally) quit drinking, I jumped in with both feet but without a compass. I simply went for it.

That was the day I emptied every closet, cupboard, and drawer in my apartment and dumped the contents onto the floor of each room. This was a few months before Marie Kondo's *The Life-Changing Magic of Tidying Up* hit bookshelves in North America, but the method was essentially the same. The neat and tidy home I'd always lived in was no more. I was left standing in a mess I didn't recognize, yet every item in it belonged to me. Staring at it all, I was overwhelmed with the task I had just created for myself. *What have I done?* When you make a mess of that size, though, you have no choice but to clean it up. It was time to get to work.

I decided to start in my bedroom—specifically, with my wardrobe. This seemed like the easiest room to tackle because, while almost every other woman I knew seemed to love clothes and accessories, I was not one of them— and never had been.

Since I was a teenager, I'd always had a uniform. Not an actual uniform like what's required in private school, but a look. It was slightly different each year. In eighth grade, I was still going through my tomboy phase, and lived in basketball jerseys and tearaway pants. In ninth grade, I swapped the jerseys for hoodies and the tearaways for jeans. Tenth grade might have been the most awkward year for me, as I made an attempt to dress a little more "girly." That look included a lot of pink that brought out the worst of my rosy complexion. By junior year, I had transformed into a surfer girl, with puka shells around my neck and a 1991 white Hyundai Excel named Roxy in my driveway. I didn't get rid of that look until I finished college in 2007, but not before getting blue waves and "island girl" translated in French tattooed on my shoulder to complete the look. Oh, the joy of being 19. And for the first five years of my career, when I worked for the government, I lived in dark slacks with dark sweaters, and a black wool peacoat with black flats.

While the look changed many times over the years, one thing did not: the fact that, at any given moment, I was probably wearing one of maybe three outfits I actually liked. By the time I emptied my closet onto the floor, these outfits consisted of jeans or khakis and a loose-fitting top or sweater. I even wore the same T-shirt and capris to the gym every other day. Altogether, I cycled through no more than 20 items of clothing (not including socks and undergarments). And I knew it. I knew I wore the same thing over and over, day in and day out. But I didn't see it until I emptied my closet and drawers and stared at the piles of fabric on the floor.

There were tank tops that matched with only a few specific sweaters. Sweaters that didn't fit right or that didn't cover up enough. Dresses I still didn't fit into, even after losing 30 pounds, but that I loved because of the way they'd hugged my curves in all the right places once upon a time. The "fat girl" clothes I thought I should keep, just in case I gained the weight back. Numerous items I'd bought because they were on sale. And then there were the government clothes, as I called them: the dark slacks and dark sweaters, and the peacoat I had always felt like I was swimming in. It was all mine, but I didn't recognize it because I didn't wear most of it.

I got rid of almost everything. I didn't hem or haw or question a single item. If I hadn't worn it in the last few months, it had to go. If it didn't fit right, it had to go. The skinnier clothes definitely had to go, because holding on to them didn't motivate me to lose more weight; it deflated me and stopped me from simply enjoying my new body and appreciating how far I had come. If I lost more weight one day, I promised myself I'd buy new dresses that would hug my new curves in all the right places. So the skinnier clothes had to go. And I knew I would never go back to the corporate world, so the government clothes could go too. I filled four black garbage bags with clothes and jackets and shoes and purses and scarves to be donated. The few items that were in rough shape went into the trash. All that was left was a closet with a dozen or so hangers in it and a three-drawer dresser that was half-full. It wasn't much, but it was what the real me would wear.

It was at this point that I decided to start keeping track of how much stuff I was getting rid of. I had kept track of my debt repayment and my workouts and my weight loss and even my months of sobriety. Now I would also keep track of this. It didn't really serve a purpose, at first, other than that it scratched my curiosity itch. After seeing 55 percent of my wardrobe go out the door, I could tell this was going to be big, and I wanted to see the numbers.

The next room I tackled was my office, which was also my living room, and technically my dining room, and even my kitchen. The open concept of my apartment meant you walked in and saw everything at once. When I emptied the cupboards, shelves, and drawers in that space, I dumped everything onto the laminate wood floor in my dining room. I had no dining table or chairs—always a surefire sign the person who lives in that apartment is single and eats on the couch. Instead, I had a room with views of the most breathtaking sunrises I've still ever seen to this day, and a giant heap of a mess in the middle of it.

That mess was harder to tackle. It made the clothes look easy. For starters, in my living room, my bookshelves had held more than just pages that contained words. They were home to dozens of trinkets. Inanimate objects that had been gifted from family and friends over the years, and even a few I'd purchased for myself. There were also projects I'd committed to tackling on the days when I bought the camera and photo albums, or paper and ink, they would require.

The books themselves were no different. My mom started reading to me before I was even born, whispering words aloud to her growing belly. She always claimed I was able to read on my own by the age of four. I only believe her because I have proof that, at age five, I catalogued my tiny collection of child-size books and created a library for all the other kids in our cul-de-sac to borrow from. The books were numbered from 1 through 10, and I used a notebook to keep track of who had what. Nobody would lose one of those prized possessions on my watch.

Like most writers, I always had a book in front of me. As a teenager, I can't remember the number of mornings I woke up for school to find my bedroom light still on and my book fallen to the floor. There was also the disastrous strep throat incident in ninth grade, when I brought an orange popsicle to bed with me and forgot to eat the other half before it could soothe my throat. I woke up with a book that had soaked up a pile of orange liquid, as well as a football-size orange stain on my white sheets. Not surprisingly, my bedding was swapped for darker colors shortly after that.

I have always loved books and loved to read. But I have also always had a bad habit of buying more books than I'll ever read in a month or even in a year. One of the many ways I mindlessly overspent money in the past was buying two books online instead of one, in order to get the total up to $25 so I could get free shipping. And even buying the first book was almost always done on impulse. I'd hear about something online or from a friend, jump on the website, then find something else that sounded good and add it to my cart, all to get that unpleasant shipping and handling fee down to $0. I did this at least once a month for probably close to a decade. At an average of $26 per order, that's $3,120 and 240 books. I would guess I read 100 of them.

The one good thing about all those moves I made in 2013 was that it showed me just how many unread books I owned but knew I didn't want to read anymore. Some were self-help books for things I no longer needed help with. Others were classics I thought I should read but which always put me to sleep. And more still were for projects I never seemed to get around to. I got rid of most of them in the course of moving—or so I thought.

By the time I tackled the books during this declutter, I found I still owned 95. Deciding what to keep and what to donate wasn't easy, but I committed to being honest with myself. Was I *really* going to read this book one day? If the answer was yes, I put it back in its place on the shelf. If the answer was no, I put it in a bag. After making this decision 95 times, I kept 8 books I'd already read but still loved, and 54 I hadn't read but still thought I would read one day. Then I donated 33 books (35 percent of my original total) to the Port Moody Public Library. If I wasn't going to read them, I wanted someone else to.

Tackling things like office supplies was easy, because I didn't have more than I needed of anything—except pens. For whatever reason, I had come into the possession of 36 pens. Nobody needed 36 pens. I kept eight, which was probably still too many, and gave the rest to a friend who was a teacher. Along with a few storage boxes, binders, and old notebooks, I removed 47 percent of my belongings from this room.

The kitchen was also a surprisingly—or perhaps not so surprisingly—simple room to put back together. It was already pretty minimal. I had what I felt was only a few too many cups, mugs, and dishes. I kept every appliance except for the blender, which I don't think I'd ever used. I also sold my juicer, after realizing how much sugar the juice was putting into my body. Natural or not, I didn't need it. I added half of my cookbooks to the bags of other books I was donating to the library. Even with the best of intentions, I had never used them. And after scaling back on the number of forks I kept in my utensil drawer, I got rid of 25 percent of what I once had.

Finally, I opened the cupboards in my bathroom and found three bags full of toiletries. I dumped the contents into the bathroom sink and watched them spill over onto the counter. There were the bottles of lotion and shower gel I had continually added to, but there were also a lot of tiny containers. Shampoos and conditioners I had picked up at various hotels. Samples that nobody ever asks to receive in the mail, but which are almost always kept so they "don't go to waste." Products passed down from family and friends who decide they don't like them but think you might. Again, even with the best of intentions, I had never used most of it. Just the way I had always worn a uniform, I'd always had a minimalist beauty routine—and this stuff was not part of it. I emptied the containers of expired or half-used products, then bagged up what could be donated to a women's shelter. Altogether, I got rid of 41 percent of my toiletries, and the rest fit into one bag that lived under the bathroom sink.

After every room was said and done, the only things I had left to go through were the boxes. The boxes I had taken out of one closet, carried to a truck, driven to a new place, carried inside, and then placed in a new closet—five times—all without ever really looking at what they contained.

The first was filled with 30 DVDs, 30 CDs, and one cassette tape. Placing 57 of those 61 items back in the box to be donated was almost like a reflex. I didn't own a device that could play their contents anymore, so they served no purpose and therefore had to go. Donating the last four took more effort: my two favorite movies from childhood, and the first two CDs I ever bought. These were things I'd imagined watching with my own kids one day, or listening to in my 80s and shaking my head at how silly it sounded now. But the world was a different place already, and all of these things could be found online. I'd never forget these films or these songs and trusted we would cross paths again. All 61 items were to go.

Only then, I hesitated. I stared at the box. It was now sitting against the wall, lined up perfectly next to the bags I'd filled, all ready to find a new home. I stared and stared, until I had to pull it back closer to me and see what was inside again. Was I really going to get rid of it all? I could hear my dad's voice. It was the same one he'd stirred up whenever he noticed I wasn't using something he and my mom had bought me. "We spent good money on that!" His guilt trips always broke my heart.

Now here I was getting ready to toss bags and boxes full of my belongings out the front door. I had spent good money on this stuff. CDs and DVDs weren't cheap, especially at the time when I'd bought some of them, when I was earning only a little more than minimum wage. The only comfort was knowing that at least those had been used. Most of the books had not. Projects gone unstarted. Clothes worn once, if at all. Toiletries stored and forgotten about until it was too late. It was all wasted. Wasted money, wasted dreams, wasted opportunities. It was almost enough to stop me from giving it away. But staring at the wasted money, dreams, and opportunities day in and day out hurt more. All items had to go.

Inside box number two, I found more boxes. Original packaging for a video game console, two modems, and a cable box, plus 14 random cables and cords. Most of these things had been free at one point, coming from cable and Internet companies or friends. I would sell the console and donate the rest.

The last box was like a secret treasure chest, disguised in cardboard, and only I knew what it contained. Underneath photo albums, my diplomas, my degree, and a stack of yearbooks, there were two glass bottles. One was an empty tequila bottle that was once filled with a smooth and warm elixir some friends brought back from Mexico as a thank you for watching their house and cats. Glued into the front of the glass was a small figurine of a man lying in a hammock, having an afternoon siesta. And that's exactly how I drank it years ago: in the afternoons, sipping it on my patio after a long day at work. *This is the life*, I thought every time it washed over my tongue.

The second bottle wasn't tequila and it wasn't from Mexico. It also wasn't empty. It was rum and it was from a local liquor store and it was cheap. It had never been opened. Much like the way I'd felt guilty about donating things I had once spent money on, I had hated the idea of wasting this rum when I first quit drinking. Sure, it was cheap. But it had once been of value to me, and it would fulfill its purpose if I let it. Weren't those the qualities the decluttering experts said every item you keep should have? Of course, now it was just a glass bottle of a liquid I couldn't put into my body—and I knew it.

I had kept the rum for the very same reason I had kept every dress, book, DVD, and cord: "just in case" I needed it. Just in case I had a bad week at work. Just in case I had my heart broken again. Just in case I needed to let loose and have a fun night. Just in case I wanted to forget. Just in case I decided this sober living thing wasn't really for me.

It was also a test—a ridiculous test I would never allow someone I loved to take, but one I gave myself nonetheless. Most days, I forgot there was a box in my bedroom closet, and that underneath the photo albums, diplomas, degree, and yearbooks inside of it, I could find an unopened bottle of white rum. But I remembered it was there whenever I found myself in one of those "just in case" situations. The bad day at work stuff, not so much. It had taken time, but I had learned the value of a workout and some fresh air to counteract that. It was mostly the hurting heart; the same hurting heart that later craved fun and excitement. Like the twitch that had prompted me to buy books whenever I wanted, I craved a drink whenever I was down. Really down, deep down. The rum was always in my back pocket. The test was to keep it there.

Going through this last box was easy, because I knew I was going to keep everything—except for the two glass bottles. They couldn't stay. The empty one had served its purpose, and I didn't need to be reminded of what that purpose once was. The full bottle needed to be emptied, only this time the contents wouldn't go down the same hole as the other bottle. It skipped my lips and went straight for the kitchen sink. As I poured, I said good-bye to the wasted money, wasted dreams, and wasted opportunities. Or maybe it was the opposite. Maybe it was the beginning of saved money, saved dreams, and saved opportunities.

By the time I was done, I had bagged up and donated 43 percent of my belongings. It was enough to fill my

Kia Rio5 from the floor of the front passenger seat to the trunk and up to the ceiling—twice. Two trips to the various donation centers later and every item was out of my life for good.

At the same time I had kept track of how many items I was getting rid of, I thought about writing down what I had kept. Sorting through and physically touching every single item I owned showed me how much I already had, which gave me a visual to remember anytime I felt like giving up on the shopping ban. But I decided to go back through it all and take a physical inventory of everything in my apartment, so I could reference how much I already had at home before going out and buying more. It was one thing to think I had an extra stick of deodorant under the sink, and another to know there were four—or none.

After that, I sold the last couple of big-ticket items I could make a few dollars from: an expensive camera I had never used, and an old laptop I had also been holding on to "just in case" my newer one died. I opened a separate savings account, where I could deposit all the money I made from selling things, as well as the money I would save each month by not buying take-out coffee, and appropriately renamed it "Shopping Ban." The money I deposited into the account would be saved all year, or I could use it to buy things on the approved shopping list.

By the end of the month, I felt good—as though I'd already accomplished a lot. My home felt lighter, somehow. There was more room to live in and more room to breathe in. If the rest of the year was as easy as this declutter and purge, I was going to have no problem walking my way to the finish line. Of course, I knew it wouldn't be. Changing a habit and routine you've spent a decade perfecting is never easy. All I had done was lay the track that would help me get to where I wanted to go. The real work was waiting around the first bend in the road. I knew it was only a matter of time before I'd get there. After all, this wasn't my first time experimenting with consuming less.

# 2

# august: changing daily habits

**months sober:** *19*
**income saved:** *19%*
**total number of belongings tossed:** *43%*

The first time I got drunk was with my biological father. It was also the first time I met him and the last time I would ever see him. I was only 12 years old.

I have intentionally chosen not to share many drinking stories on my blog. It was never that I was afraid of what people would think of me, but that I didn't want to be a source of entertainment. I've always hated the idea of sharing this story, in particular, because I didn't want my

*family* to be a source of entertainment. It's also not indic-
ative of my upbringing. Alas, it's the truth, and it turned
me on to drinking at an age when most kids are focused
on playing with friends or winning their soccer game.

My mom and biological father were never married.
Honestly, they were barely even a couple. A handful of
dates led to one positive pregnancy test that changed my
mom's life forever. He wanted nothing to do with the situation, and quite literally fled the country, moving to the
United States before I was even born. She accepted the
news and chose to be my mother and for me to be her
daughter. I emphasize the word *chose* because, in my eyes,
that's a decision she had the right to make (although she
would tell you I was a gift). She chose for the two of us to
become a family, then she later chose my stepdad to join
us. As a note: I will refer to my stepdad as my dad throughout this book, because that's exactly who and what he is.

Looking back, one of the things I'm most grateful for
about the way I was raised is that my mom never introduced me to anyone she dated, until she met my dad. Even
then, after seven years of it just being the two of us, I can't
say I was particularly open to the idea. Actually, I hated
that someone was coming into our apartment and taking
up the space in her bed that I crawled into whenever I
had a bad dream. That was my pillow. My blanket. My
bed. My mom.

My mom and dad met in 1992, and by 1995 they were
married and had grown our family from three to five.
Being eight years older than my sister, Alli, and ten years
older than my brother, Ben, came with unique challenges.
Our dad sailed up and down the coast of British Columbia
with the Canadian Coast Guard for half the year, during
which time my role shifted from big sister to third parent.

I picked "the kids" up from school, took them to sports, cooked dinner, did laundry, helped clean the house, and so on. While some teenagers might reject or rebel against these duties, I stepped into the role proudly.

When I was 12, my biological father contacted my mom to let her know he was coming to Victoria—my hometown and the place they had first met. His own mom and brother still lived there, so he was coming to see them but wanted to know if the three of us could also have dinner. She asked me how I felt about it. The answer: indifferent. I was curious, of course. As far as growing up with a single parent concerned me, I'd always thought I had the best of one. My mom worked hard to make a life for us and, between her and my dad, I never went without anything and always knew I was loved. But still, I wondered who this mythical person was who helped create me. We agreed to meet him.

My memory of that night is clear but full of confusion. Clear, because I can still play back every moment, the same way you remember the awkwardness of a first date or first kiss. But full of confusion, because I'll never understand what he was thinking when he put me in the situations he did.

The conversation over our meal was casual. Where are you living now? What do you do for work? How's your family? Surface-level stuff. I quietly listened as they talked to each other, talked about me, and then talked to me. I didn't know what to say—what 12-year-old would? Up until that point, my life had revolved around friends, books, basketball, and crushes on boys. *Did he really want to hear about that?*

Instead, I stayed silent and stared at him as they talked, examining every detail of his face and comparing it to my own. He had blonde hair. I had blonde hair. My mom, dad, Alli, and Ben all had dark brown hair, so I was always the odd one out. *He made this part of me*, I thought. We shared the same nose. I also noticed that his top lip thinned as he smiled, threw his head back, and laughed. I had always hated that mine disappeared when I did the same. Now I knew who to blame.

As we were getting ready to leave, he asked my mom if he could take me downtown for ice cream. My biological father was a freelance photographer and wanted to take some pictures of the city he had once called home. "Get the whole vibe, ya!" This was how he spoke: using words like *vibe* and *groovy* and *man* and *ya!* in an accent that was part English and part South African. I didn't know what to make of it, except that it sounded worldly to my adolescent ears. My mom asked if I wanted to go. It felt more awkward to say no, so I got into his car and we headed south on Quadra Street toward the Inner Harbour.

What I didn't understand then was that he never planned to take me out for ice cream. Instead, after I listened to him grumble and swear about not being able to find parking downtown, he walked us into the oldest pub in Bastion Square and sat me down at the bar. There, he asked the bartender to look after me, then winked, smiled, and vanished around a corner.

He left me there for what felt like hours but was probably more like 30 minutes. In that time, the bartender served me what I later learned were two lime margaritas. The first one tasted like a Slurpee from 7-Eleven. I sipped it hurriedly while staring at the television, hoping that the faster I finished, the sooner we could leave. By the time he put the second one in front of me, everything looked a little glossy and my insides felt warm. When my biological father finally returned from catching up with friends, he could tell I was drunk. "A coffee and whisky should fix her right up, man!" he yelled to the bartender. I took one sip, slowly spat it back into the black mug, and asked if he could take me home.

That car ride can still be described as the most uncomfortable situation I've ever been in. For 20 minutes, he asked me questions like, "What's your stepdad like, anyway?" and "Do you think you, me, and your mom will ever be a family?" I stared out the window and watched cars and houses blur past us, as I bit my tongue to help me hold back tears, and prayed to whatever god was out there that I would get home to my family soon. Suddenly, all I could think about was how I never wanted to live without Alli and Ben. My half-siblings. My only siblings.

My mom must have been sitting by the front window, watching out for me, because in the same minute we pulled into the driveway, she opened the front door and walked outside. After I got out of the car, he gave her a wave and sped off in the old and rusty white Buick he'd borrowed from his own mother. She stood at the top of the stairs and stared down at me as I staggered up the driveway toward her. The glass stucco siding cut into my hand as I held myself up against the house and slowly took each one of the 10 stairs to the top. When I finally made it to the door, I could see on her face that my mom was horrified. It was the first time she'd ever looked at me that way, but it wouldn't be the last. I walked into the house, still using the walls to hold myself up, until I got to my room, let go, and collapsed onto my bed.

I don't know all the details about what happened after that. All I remember is lying on my bed and listening to my mom yell into the phone in the kitchen. She called my biological father, then she called the pub that had served me the alcohol, and then she threatened to call the police. The sick joke was that his brother was a constable at the police station attached to the municipal hall my mom worked at. Proof of how small Victoria was. I had never met the brother, which was perhaps also proof of how big a small city can be. But I knew he was going to hear about this the next day. She said so on the phone.

I listened from my bed and watched the posters of Jonathan Taylor Thomas on the wall spin around the room, until I closed my eyes and slipped away from it all.

Perhaps the most unfortunate part of that story isn't that it happened, but that I wore it like a badge of adulthood for years after.

In Victoria, the public school system used to be divided in such a way that you only went to two schools: elementary school (from kindergarten to seventh grade) and high school (from eighth grade to senior year). Shortly after my first drinking experience, I turned 13 and entered high school. There, I formed a new group of friends, which mostly consisted of girls in eighth grade and boys in ninth grade.

As most young angsty teens do, we exchanged all the war stories from our childhoods. Many of my new friends had parents who were divorced and some had stepparents they claimed to hate. A few also had parents who abused alcohol and drugs enough that even their own kids knew it was unhealthy. But no one was using these things themselves yet, except for a few boys who would steal cigarettes or a single can of beer from the fridge. As I learned all this, I knew I had an opportunity to stand out.

Growing up, I had never been particularly good at anything. I was on the basketball team in sixth and seventh grade, but typically only got a few minutes of playing time each game. I was often picked last for teams in gym class. I also wasn't exactly "good looking" then, with hair that was cut too short and extra weight around my stomach and hips. Nothing about me seemed worth paying attention to. However, I did have a one-up on most of my new friends: I was the first one of us who had gotten drunk.

"This summer, I went out with my real dad and got so wasted!" I shared, like it was the highlight. Then I described the drinks in detail, as though I were a cocktail expert, and finished by saying, "We should drink together sometime!" And just like that, I was not only "in" with these people, I was one of the leaders of the pack.

Soon, we started drinking every weekend. One of the boys in ninth grade had a friend with an older brother who was happy to buy us alcohol on Fridays. A group of 10 or 15 of us would meet at the bleachers by the school and wait for our special delivery. The minivan appeared at the same time each week—six o'clock in the dark winter nights, eight o'clock in the spring—and we spent the next few hours sipping on two-liter bottles of hard cider, prancing around the baseball diamond like we owned the place.

I didn't know it then, but I would spend the next 14 years drinking for all the wrong reasons. I would drink to feel like a cooler version of myself—someone people might actually like. I would use alcohol as a lubricant for awkward social situations, especially dating and sex. And I would drink to numb my insecurities. But I didn't know that then. All I knew was that I was good at it. I was good at finding alcohol. I was good at drinking alcohol. I was good at keeping up with the boys and never getting sick from alcohol. I was good at partying.

I went from drinking once or twice a week in high school, to drinking three or four nights a week in my 20s, and getting blackout drunk almost every single time.

There were two different kinds of blackouts. First, there were the nights when I would only lose an hour or two. I would have to ask my friends what time we left the party or what my crush had said to me in text messages. I deleted all traces of those conversations before I went to bed, because I didn't want proof of the ridiculous things I might have texted in the morning. Those blackouts weren't so bad; losing an hour or two felt okay.

Then there were the nights when I would forget everything *after* the first hour or two. I would gulp down all the alcohol I had like it was going to be taken away from me. My last memory was always something fun, like singing in the street on the way to a party or arriving and hugging all my friends. Then I would wake up in the morning, usually in my bed but sometimes on someone's couch, with six or more hours of lost time to account for.

I hated that kind of blackout. I hated the feeling of wondering what I might have drunk, snorted, eaten, or acted out. I hated the pit in my stomach that warned me I might have done or said something stupid, and potentially altered one of my relationships. I hated not knowing. And yet, I continued to drink this way for 14 years.

I read somewhere that people attempt to quit things up to a dozen times before they finally quit for good. This was certainly true for my drinking.

The first time I thought about getting sober was the morning after a Christmas/good-bye party at a friend's house. She was heading off to Thailand for four months. To send her off in style, we drank Thai beer and spiced rum and eggnog—a disgusting combination, but one that seemed appropriate to our 20-year-old selves. Fifteen or more of us slid all over her kitchen floor, dancing in our socks while her dad's band played for us live.

I woke up fully clothed in bed the next morning with no recollection of how I had gotten there. It took four days and dozens of conversations with friends to figure out what had happened. Apparently, I had called a cab, then fallen asleep on the sidewalk waiting for it. Some time later, my friend's parents found me, picked me up from the concrete, and put me in the back of their van. I must have been coherent enough to give them directions to my own parents' house, where they carried me in and put me to bed. I remembered none of it. Anyone could have picked me up off the street that night.

Early in the new year, I wrote a card to the parents who found me and thanked them for their help. I also expressed the weighted guilt and distress that comes from not knowing exactly what happened, and told them I planned to never drink again. "It's been three weeks and I haven't had a drop," I wrote matter-of-factly. But I started drinking again shortly after, and didn't make another attempt to quit for five years.

In 2011, my New Year's resolution was to not drink for an entire year. I think I lasted 23 days. In February of that year, I took a leave of absence from my job and flew across the country in an attempt to make a new life for myself. Instead, I drank away all of my savings in just eight weeks and spent my last $350 on a flight home to Victoria with close to $30,000 of consumer debt. At that point I *had* to slow down and drink less often. But whenever I could afford a $10 bottle of wine, I bought it and drank every last sip—usually within an hour's time.

In the summer of 2012, a long-term relationship ended in a particularly devastating way. I partied harder than ever to forget about it. But as the summer went on, I knew my drinking days were numbered. Just like the gut feeling in 2011 that told me I was getting closer and closer to being maxed out, a little voice kept telling me I couldn't do this to myself anymore. The reasons why I was drinking heavily had become so obvious that I could no longer ignore them. I drank to feel like a cooler version of myself. I used alcohol as a lubricant for awkward social situations, especially dating and sex. And I drank to numb my pain and insecurities. Nothing had changed since I was a kid.

In late August of that year, I was offered a full-time managing editor position at a financial startup in Toronto. The CEO had read my blog, liked my work, and knew I loved the city. "Want to come out here?" she asked. Little did she know I was desperate for a new life. I accepted her offer, quit my stable job with the government, packed my belongings into two duffel bags, and jumped on a plane three weeks later.

I celebrated my arrival by going out and partying with friends. Then we celebrated a couple birthdays, and I even partied with my new co-workers one night. But at the same time, the voice in my head got louder. I knew exactly what I was doing: pretending I was happy and excited to be in Toronto, while trying to mask how deeply I was still affected by the ending of what can still be described as one of the most meaningful relationships of my young adult life. I didn't want to feel the pain, but even alcohol couldn't stop me from hurting anymore.

The hurt took over every aspect of my life, and threw all the good habits I'd created out the door too. I was spending more money again and making bad food choices. And I couldn't remember the last time I had gone for a run or to the gym. By the time the seasons changed over from summer to fall, I knew the only way I could turn things around was to quit drinking once and for all. This time, I even wrote about it on my blog, in a post titled "I'm Done Making Excuses (Again)." I thought writing about it and hitting "Publish" would force me to stay accountable. It had worked when I was maxed out and when I decided to get healthy, so it would help me quit drinking too, right?

Forty-five days later, I drank two beers at a concert and went on a six-week bender that included: blacking out for most of my first trip to New York City; finding myself in a number of uncomfortable situations with men; racking up a $450 tab at a bar; and waking up one morning to discover I had somehow lost the jeans I'd been wearing and come home in a dress.

I attempted to quit drinking many times, but I wasn't done until I was really done; that day finally came when I was 27. After waking up from yet another blackout, and remembering only fragments of yet another problematic situation the night before, I knew I was done. The situation hadn't been more troublesome than any of the others before it, but I was ready for it to be my last. I could only wake up and say, "I can't keep doing this" so many times, and now I had reached my quota.

The toughest part of quitting drinking wasn't that I couldn't drink—it was that I couldn't drink when I had to face those awkward social situations, or felt insecure or rejected, which, it turned out, was often. It was the times when a feeling I'd grown accustomed to hating and then masking with alcohol could no longer be covered up. The bad weeks at work that were only forgotten after an entire bottle of wine, or two. The cold shoulders from men that were rehashed with friends over four tall cans of hard cider and six shots of whatever was cheap at the bar. I couldn't drown it away anymore. I had to feel the discomfort, crave the drink, then push past it and find a new way to handle the situation.

Not even two years later, I was only one month into the shopping ban when I started to see the similarities between giving up alcohol and giving up take-out coffee. While the drink of choice was seemingly harmless, forgoing my sometimes twice-daily latte felt like giving up my evening glass(es) of wine. I never imagined I would crave the coffee as much as I did.

I thought about lattes first thing in the morning on days when I woke up so tired I could barely open my eyes. Somehow, getting dressed and going downstairs to the coffee shop in my building seemed easier than walking into my own kitchen to brew a pot. I thought about them again midmorning when I wanted to take a break from work. The voice in my head told me I deserved it. And I thought about them before running errands or going on a road trip. I didn't know how many habits I had that centered on drinking take-out coffee until I wasn't allowed to buy it. Each time I craved it, I had to stand in the moment, pay attention to what had triggered the craving, and change my reaction.

Giving up take-out coffee was obviously a lot easier than giving up booze. I would never, and could never, pretend otherwise. When I craved a latte in the morning, all I had to do was walk into my kitchen and fill my French press. Sometimes I treated myself to a bottle of hazelnut syrup and attempted to make a homemade latte substitute. And before getting into my car for long periods of time, I would fill my water bottle and travel coffee mug and take them with me. After I did these things enough times, they became new habits. By mid-August, I was feeling good about the changes I was making.

The same hadn't always been true when I was getting sober—and it couldn't always be said for my shopping ban, even now. For years, I had thought I needed alcohol to make my life better, the same way I thought buying things made my life better. I didn't think about shopping every day. I didn't even think about shopping every week. But suddenly I'd find myself craving something I hadn't wanted seconds before.

I'd hear about a good book and suddenly find myself on the retailer web page. Or I'd walk into a store to replace my mascara, then notice the rows of eyeshadows telling me I probably wasn't wearing the right color and should try something new. I had no idea what BB cream was (and I still don't really know), but every advertisement told me it would make my skin perfect, so I started to think I needed that. Then I noticed that the scarf next to the hooded sweatshirt I was considering buying (from the approved shopping list) looked like it was my style. Maybe I needed that too! Of course, I didn't need, and didn't buy, any of it.

The toughest part of not being allowed to buy anything new wasn't that I couldn't buy anything new—it was having to physically confront my triggers and change my reaction to them. It always felt like the minute I for-got about the shopping ban was the same minute I felt like shopping again. It was like an ex I just couldn't get away from.

In each instance, I would pause, take in my surround-ings, and try to figure out why I was thinking about mak-ing a purchase. Sometimes it was because my fingers were within walking distance of a computer, so opening an online shopping website was easy. Other times it was the merchandising or smell of the store. More often, though, it was simply because that was what I had always done. In the past, whenever I wanted something, I bought it—no questions asked, budget and savings goals be damned. To combat these impulses now, the only thing I could ever think to do was remember how much stuff I had gotten rid of and how much I still had at home. It was enough. I had enough.

It wasn't until I found myself in these situations that I realized the shopping ban was going to be more difficult than I'd thought. This was going to be about more than just not spending money—I'd be changing the habits and routines I'd spent years perfecting.

Every study I've read about how long it takes to change a habit gives a different answer. Some say it can be done in 21 days, others 66 days or even 12 weeks. For me, nearly two months into the ban, I was still constantly identify-ing my spending triggers and pushing past them, while at the same time trying to understand why they existed in the first place. This didn't—and still doesn't—surprise me. Ask any addict how long it took them to stop feeling like their drug of choice (whether it be alcohol, drugs, food, or anything else) was the one thing that would help them through any situation, and I can guarantee no one will say 21 days.

By the end of August, I was 56 days into the shopping ban and still felt my bad spending habits lurking beneath my good intentions. I had learned what most of my daily habits were, but I was about to find out my spending decisions were a lot more emotional than I thought.

# 3

# september: breaking up with retail therapy

**months sober:** *20*
**income saved:** *12% (traveled all month)*
**confidence I can complete this project:** *60%*

When you hear the word *shopaholic*, you might picture a woman in high heels carrying handfuls of shopping bags full of clothes, shoes, and makeup. That's what I have always pictured, likely because that's what the media and popular stories have shown us to be true. There are books about shopaholics. Entire book series about shopaholics.

Movies about shopaholics. And the picture on the cover is always the same: a woman in high heels carrying handfuls of shopping bags full of clothes, shoes, and makeup.

For that reason, I have never identified with the term. Aside from the car I had financed, most of my previous debt was a result of dining out and partying—living a lifestyle I couldn't afford because my credit cards made it affordable. It was not all a result of shopping. I would occasionally hit the mall with friends, but it wasn't one of my usual pastimes. I did some mindless spending, buying books I didn't really need, and going into a store for two things and walking out with five. But I didn't wear high heels, and I never brought home bags full of clothes, shoes, and makeup. So I wasn't a shopaholic—right?

It's easy to look at a picture of a stereotype, point your finger at it, and say, "I don't look like that, so I'm not that way." By announcing this, we somehow feel better about ourselves, even though we've just shamed every other person who does fit under that umbrella. I may not have identified as a shopaholic, but there was no doubt I was a compulsive shopper.

I was a compulsive binge consumer of everything, really, including food and alcohol. I didn't even know how to stop myself from binging on television for hours on end, something I wasted all the rest of my time in my 20s doing when I wasn't out actually getting wasted. I didn't identify as an alcoholic, either, though a medical professional likely would have identified me as such at one time in my life. I often lied about how many drinks I had, I lied about how much I spent, and I lied about how I paid for it all—always with cash, never with credit, because "I could afford it." When it came to my shopping, I told all the same lies and made all the same excuses.

I was also someone who, on occasion, fell victim to the retail therapy trap and bought stuff in an attempt to make myself feel better. Drinking was my usual go-to. But when big things happened—the things that pulled the rug out from under me, causing me to fall to my knees and have to shakily try to get back up—that was when I did the most damage to my finances through purchases I couldn't really afford. For me, those big things were usually breakups.

A few weeks before I decided to do the shopping ban, I started seeing someone new. Andrew and I had met when I was in Toronto in June. I was still working for the Toronto-based financial startup I had left my government job for in 2012 (though I now worked remotely and traveled back to the city often), and he was an accountant. We bonded over our love of numbers and spreadsheets, then quickly fell into a comfortable groove and made each other laugh. Despite the fact that we lived thousands of miles apart, we had an instant connection we thought was worth exploring.

The honeymoon phase was as wonderful as the name suggests. Because Andrew was in a different time zone, three hours ahead of me, I woke up every morning to a thoughtful text message that ended with a heart or a kiss. We would talk on the phone for hours, late into the night, and have Skype dates where we would eat dinner and watch the same black-and-white movies at the same time. After only a month of this, he asked if I was interested in dating anyone else or could we be exclusive. I was floating. If we'd been together in person, I imagined he would've picked me up from the ground and twirled us three times, and our romantic black-and-white-movie-style kiss would've sealed the deal.

Aside from how sweet he was, one of the things I appreciated most about Andrew was that he wasn't afraid to ask tough questions and start difficult conversations—about the things many people avoid, especially in the beginning of a relationship. We shared our salaries and net worths. We talked about our beliefs, both religious and political. We had numerous discussions about my sobriety and what it meant for me. (He drank socially, which I'd learned would probably be true of any partner I had.) And we talked at length about our past relationships, getting to the root of where things had gone wrong and why they ultimately ended.

Andrew had always been honest about the fact that he was divorced. He had been with his ex for more than a decade, and they'd gotten married because that seemed like the next logical step. It quickly fell apart, however, and ended with her cheating on him. He could've blamed the whole situation on her. Most people would have. I probably would have, if I had been in his shoes. Instead, he talked about his part in the unfolding—how he had taken the relationship for granted, and how he would shut down during any conflict. From this, he had learned vows were just words; actions were what made them commitments.

During our conversations, his personal revelations had a tendency to shake me up—not because of anything he said about me, but because his stories made me think of my own. I would have flashbacks to the last serious relationship I was in, and I'd remember things I had blocked out. Images of my ex, Chris, pushing me onto the bed, then shoving a pillow over my face while yelling at me. Or pinning me against the wall when I tried to leave, and taking the key and locking me out of our apartment so I couldn't get back in. For the first time in years, I also remembered some of my reactions to these things. They were not pretty, and I was not perfect. I had shoved all of these memories into a box—this one stored in the back corner of my mind, hidden behind memories of all the good things that had happened since we'd broken up: finally going back to school, getting my degree in communications, landing a job across the country, paying off my debt, taking control of my health, quitting drinking, and so on. My conversations with Andrew helped me see the truth, though: Chris wasn't the only one to blame for our unfolding. I had become the worst version of myself in that relationship too.

Whenever I made a discovery like that, I felt as though Andrew was holding up a mirror in front of me. Through our conversations, he helped me see things about myself that were probably painfully obvious to everyone around me but that I had never noticed before. Like him, I learned I had a tendency to shut down during conflict. I also gave up my interests and opinions too easily. I accepted whatever love was given to me, thinking that was as good as it was going to get. And after my relationship ended with Chris, I started telling myself I was intentionally choosing to stay single so I could focus on myself and my work. But when a mirror is held up in front of you, you are forced to see the truth: I had shut myself off from the idea of dating, too afraid to go through all of that again. I let my friends in, but I had my guard up so high that guys couldn't even see me. Dating simply wasn't an option. I wasn't an option.

Andrew learned all of these things about me, as I learned them about myself, and none of it seemed to scare him off. In fact, in the midst of these deep conversations, he made plans. We made plans. Real plans. Like mapping out the dates we could visit each other in the next six months (one trip every six weeks) and deciding how we would split the cost of our long-distance relationship (the person flying would pay the airfare, the person hosting would pay for everything else). I missed him every day, but I didn't have any doubts. It felt like this could really be something.

I flew out to spend a week with him over Labor Day, and we immediately fell into a routine that would've made anyone watching think we'd been together for years. We glided around each other in the kitchen, him cooking and me cleaning. As we walked through the grocery store, I reminded him of all the things we needed that he'd forgotten to write down. We held hands or rubbed each other's backs whenever we were side by side. Even the way we curled up on the couch looked like two puzzle pieces that had finally been put together. Everything seemed perfect—*this could really be something*, I thought—until the night before I left.

Andrew was unusually quiet. He took his familiar position on the couch, with his head on my lap and arms wrapped around me. But he said nothing as we watched a movie, and nothing after it ended, and nothing as we crawled into bed. We didn't have sex that night. He didn't spoon me or even pull me in closer to him, like he had done every night before. Instead, he curled up on one side with his back turned to me. This was his wall. He had put up his wall. In the face of a conflict he apparently wasn't comfortable approaching, he had shut down and now there was a wall up between us. I lay on my back and stared at the ceiling, thinking of what I could say to break it down. *Should I ask him if everything is okay? Should I say nothing and curl up next to him? Should I just make a move and see if sex will help?* I decided the second option was a good start, but before I could move or say a word, he started snoring. I had missed my opportunity to break the wall down. And with that, I curled into a ball so our backs were to each other, and let a quiet stream of tears fall from my eyes. I didn't know you could feel alone while you were in bed with someone, until that moment.

During our drive to the airport in the morning, I knew it was over. I didn't know why, I didn't know what had happened, but I did know this was the end. We didn't look like two people who had just spent a week together. Instead, we acted stiff and our conversation sounded more like two colleagues making small talk after a conference.

"Did you enjoy your time here?" he asked.

"Yes, I'm glad I came."

I bit my tongue when I felt tears begin to well up in my eyes. I wanted to ask him so many questions, but I was terrified of the responses. The thought of having to deal with another heartbreak hurt enough. He knew it. I'd let my guard down with him, and he knew it. I wasn't ready to get hurt again. So I shut down. It wasn't the grown-up thing to do, but that's what I did. I put my own wall up and I said nothing.

When we got to the airport, he didn't undo his seat belt and get out to hug me. Instead, he leaned over and kissed me. It felt forced, and I instantly wished we could take it back. Then I grabbed my bags and said good-bye, knowing it would probably be the last time we ever saw each other.

Over the next few weeks, Andrew and I continued to communicate over text message, but it wasn't the same. I would wake up every morning hoping to see one of his thoughtful notes with a kiss, but they were never there. I always probed him about his day, his work, his family and friends. His responses were short, which often hurt more than not hearing from him at all. I was still too scared to ask what was wrong, though. I wasn't ready to hear the answer, so I didn't ask the question. The only thing that helped me forget how lonely it was to be in a practically nonexistent text message relationship was my busy travel schedule.

From Andrew's, I went up to Kingston, Ontario, for my boss's wedding. Immediately after that, I flew back to Vancouver, got in my car, and picked up my friend Kasey for a girls' weekend. We drove the I-5 down to Portland, Oregon, where we spent three days drinking coffee and eating, crossing off restaurants like they were on our list of things to do before we died. Coffee at Stumptown, brunch at Tasty n Alder, dinner at Pok Pok, and ice cream at Salt & Straw. If we really had died that weekend, we would've gone out with full bellies and smiles tattooed on our faces. I also would've died with my phone in my hand, because I couldn't stop looking at it, wondering if Andrew was ever going to send one of his usual text messages again. I hated that I was in this position. I hated that I had become the girl who was sitting around, waiting for a guy. But I waited and waited and checked my phone for his messages. They never came through.

Two days after Kasey and I returned from Portland, I drove back to the airport and took three more planes down to New Orleans for a conference. (The curse of living on the west coast of Canada is that it always takes multiple flights to get anywhere else.) I sent Andrew a message to let him know that I had arrived safely—something he always asked me to do when I traveled—and that we were in the same time zone again. His replies seemed warmer—our conversation lasted longer. I eventually asked if we could talk on the phone, and he agreed. But our warm greetings lasted only a few minutes before he grew cold again and I'd had enough. Screw the walls we had both put up. "What is going on with you?" I demanded. "Why are you so distant?" In a few brief sentences, he said what I had known since the night before I left his place: He didn't want to be in a serious relationship. Even though I had felt it coming for weeks, the words made it real, and I was devastated. I spent the first 24 hours of my time in New Orleans in my hotel room, curled up under the covers.

When I eventually got out of bed, I was grateful to be in a new city with good friends from all over the country. In between conference sessions and activities, we walked all throughout the French Quarter and up to Louis Armstrong Park. We left behind rings of powdered sugar at our table after sipping coffee and devouring too many orders of beignets outside Café du Monde in the morning. We ate muffulettas from Central Grocery & Deli for lunch, and jambalaya and po'boys for dinner. And, of course, there was jazz—so much jazz—on Bourbon Street at night.

Still, as grateful as I was to be in NOLA, and to be there with friends, I could never seem to distract myself long enough to make the pain go away. I found myself constantly wanting to do anything at all that might brighten my day, or lighten some of the load I was carrying around with me. Often, the "anything" I resorted to was thinking about something I could buy. Because that's what happens when things hurt. You try to fix the hurt, and solve every other problem in your life too—even the things that aren't really problems at all.

It started with a daily planner. I hadn't properly used a daily planner in years. With the best of intentions, I would buy one and use it for the first three weeks of January, then forget about it until May. At that point, I would pick it up and think, *Well, that was a waste of money, there's no point starting almost halfway through the year,* and throw it out. As an adult, I had always had this relationship with daily planners. But now that I was back home from New Orleans and craving a fresh start, I needed one. I really needed it. And this was the perfect planner! It had just the right amount of space to write down both my personal and work tasks, and quotes to help me stay motivated, and blank pages in the back where I could keep track of the books I'd read. It was also an 18-month daily planner, so I could start now and use it all the way to the end of 2015. It was perfect. It felt like it had been made for me.

Then I began to notice how much I hated my clothes. Everything felt old and shabby. In turn, I felt old and shabby. The women I saw walking around my neighborhood or through the grocery store looked so much more put together. They looked happy. I looked old and shabby. I started browsing online stores for anything that could make me look more put together. I found shirts that looked more grown-up, and pants that weren't jeans, because all I ever wore was jeans and how unprofessional was that? *I should also start wearing dresses,* I thought. I had always hated dresses, but the women I saw wearing them looked so cute, and it was such a simple outfit to put together. *Hey, look! There's an empire-waist dress that would look great on me. Maybe I should get it in two different colors.*

Aside from the planner and the clothes, I thought about buying books constantly. There was also a handmade mug I imagined sipping coffee from each morning, and a rug I thought would keep my feet warmer in the kitchen, and a chef's knife because I didn't own a single sharp knife and how could I cook another meal without one? The biggest problem to fix would then be the replacement of my cell phone, because mine was old and slow and sometimes shut itself off, which always filled me with unnecessary rage. I *needed* it. Replacing my cell phone would remove a daily annoyance and make my life so much better. I deserved to have my life be so much better. It wasn't until I physically added the new phone to the shopping cart on my cell phone provider's website and looked at the total that I realized what was about to happen. If I hit the submit button, I was going to be buying something and, therefore, breaking the shopping ban. Having the ban loom over me not only stopped me from potentially wasting hundreds and thousands of dollars, it also forced me to pause and question what I was doing. This was something I had never done before, especially during a breakdown.

I didn't buy any of the things I wanted to that month. I emptied the shopping carts and closed the tabs in my browser and didn't buy a single thing. But old me would have. Old me *had*.

It was almost six years to the day that Chris and I had broken up. Our relationship could have been described in only a few words: turbulent, tumultuous, toxic. We were both addicts who abused alcohol, drugs, and each other—emotionally, verbally, and physically. It took a long time to see how bad things really were, because in between all the abuse was a lot of affection and promise. We would pick at each other's insecurities for weeks, have explosive arguments, then apologize and express deep and tender love for one another. I knew it wasn't healthy and that it couldn't last forever. But every time I thought about leaving, Chris begged for forgiveness. He promised to be better, listed all the ways he would be more helpful, and said he would do anything to make it work. I don't know that I ever truly believed him, but I wanted to. I thought about the special language we had and the plans we'd made and the physical chemistry between us that somehow didn't fade no matter how bad things were. I wanted to believe he would help make it work, so I forgave him. When the tables were turned, he forgave me. We forgave each other. And then a few weeks later, we'd have another fight, I'd think about leaving again, and the cycle would start all over.

The same way it took a dozen or more attempts for me to quit drinking, I made at least that many attempts to walk away from our relationship. When Chris and I finally separated, I got an apartment I would live alone in for the first time. I'd moved out of my parents' house when I was 18 years old, and had always had a roommate or lived with a boyfriend. I had also always filled my home with secondhand furniture (often free) and other household items gifted from family and friends. Aside from my OCD tendencies, which forced me to line everything up and keep it neat and tidy, I had never cared about how things looked or where they came from or if anything matched. This time was different.

In the past, I had moved out for specific reasons. To gain some independence from my parents. To save on rent. To find a roommate who better suited my lifestyle. After my breakup with Chris, though, I *had* to build a new life for myself—one that didn't include Chris. I wanted it to look like the exact opposite of everything I had just walked away from. I wanted peace and serenity and comfort. I wanted it to feel like a home. So I did the thing I knew could help me create the peaceful and serene and comfortable home I desperately wanted: I went shopping.

At the first store, I spent $1,300 on a brand-new soft green microfiber sofa set for the living room. Then I picked out a black coffee table, side table, bookshelf, and mirror, for another $700. I filled the shelves with books and knick-knacks—curated objects found in overpriced stores that screamed "me." I bought and hung pictures I loved, without worrying what anyone else's opinions of them would be. And I treated myself to all new bedding. My bed would be my sanctuary, my safe place to retreat at night. Altogether, I spent more than $3,000 in less than a week. And I wasn't done there.

To go along with the furniture, I decided this was a good time to replace most of my wardrobe. A few months later, I financed a brand-new car to the tune of $15,000. The justifications for that decision were haunting. Shortly after Chris and I had first gotten together, the 1991 Hyundai Excel I had been driving since high school died. The cost to fix it far outweighed the value of my dear Roxy. Also, Chris had a truck and said I could use it anytime. I trusted him, decided not to fix Roxy, and instead said good-bye and sent her to car heaven (the junkyard). Of course, it didn't take long for me to learn that Chris's offer was conditional. I could use his truck if I filled it up with gas. I could use his truck if I was only going out for an hour or two. I could use his truck if I didn't hang out with any male friends in that time. For that last point, he would berate me when I came home, as though he thought his words would cause me to confess my sins. So when I was finally out on my own, I decided I needed a car. I needed a car that came without strings attached. "Cars give you freedom," I said over and over again, to anyone who would listen. That was all I wanted: to be free.

In three months I had pieced together my new life. I had an apartment filled with matching furniture, a closet full of new clothes, and a brand-new car. From the outside, it looked perfect—and it had only taken three months to create. I was finally free. Except I wasn't free, because my new life had cost close to $20,000. It was all paid for with credit, the debt was mine, and I would carry the weight of it for many years. There was nothing free about that.

My breakup with Andrew didn't compare to what I had gone through with Chris in 2008. Our relationship was shorter. It wasn't turbulent, tumultuous, or toxic. And we didn't spend months wavering on our decision, continuing to use and abuse each other until one of us finally waved a white flag and said enough was enough. On paper, it didn't compare at all. But it still hurt. I had finally taken my guard down and let a guy see me as an option. I had let myself see dating as an option again. And then it wasn't an option with Andrew any longer, and it hurt.

I don't remember how much it hurt with Chris, because back then I numbed myself. I numbed my sadness with food, and my emptiness with stuff. And I numbed my loneliness by hosting lots of parties at my new apartment and leaving no bottle behind. I didn't feel anything, because I didn't let myself feel anything. If a pinch or sting ever came through my skin, I immediately picked up my phone and invited friends over to drink. I was constantly applying this salve, so the problem never healed, but it didn't get infected either. I didn't realize this pattern until my breakup with Andrew. This time, I couldn't numb myself. I had to experience every excruciating feeling.

When I finally got home from my month full of travel, I did just that. At night, I crawled into bed feeling so alone that my bones physically ached. In the morning, I would go about my regular routine and remind myself things would feel normal again soon. I did some decluttering, getting rid of more toiletries I never used and a few items of clothing I hadn't worn since my first purge. I got more comfortable in my space, and moved things around my apartment to make it more functional. I went hiking with friends on the weekends. I kept living. I felt things and I kept living. I didn't numb myself with food or alcohol. And I didn't shop. It wasn't going to help. It had never actually helped before, and it wasn't going to help this time either.

On my blog, I announced that I had survived the first three months of the shopping ban, but that wasn't the real thing to celebrate. The real thing to celebrate was that I had felt things and I kept living.

# 4

# october:
# growing up
# and apart

**months sober:** *21*
**income saved:** *23%*
**total number of belongings tossed:** *50%*

In early October, I took pictures of my apartment as it looked then and pasted them next to pictures taken after my initial declutter and purge in July. The differences were minimal at best. I had pared down my wardrobe further, donated more books, and moved a few things around. My bulletin board had somehow exploded, with papers pinned on top of more papers, but everything else looked generally the same. At the request of a handful of people who had asked if I could show them what my home looked like and explain whether or not my decluttering efforts had worked, I shared the pictures on my blog. The post took readers on a tour of my apartment and showed that yes, in fact, the efforts had worked. My home was clutter-free. Everything had a place and it all lined up. I was happy to share this, and most readers were happy to see it. A few, however, were not.

When it comes to my blog, there are two rules I have always tried to live by. The first is that if someone takes the time to write a comment and share part of themselves with me, in return, I will take the time to write a thoughtful reply. I don't always reply to new comments that come in on older posts, but if you comment on something I have recently published, I will do my best to get back to you. I do this not only because I respect people's time, but because I love the conversations we have in that space, and I am so incredibly grateful for every connection we can make in this world.

The second rule I have always lived by is something I once heard at a conference, which is that a blog is not a democracy. The blogger is allowed to control the conversation, to some degree, and should. That doesn't mean deleting comments that challenge your opinion or make you think. Those are actually some of the best comments, because they push you to open your mind and expand your viewpoint. But it does mean deleting comments from Internet trolls—people whose sole purpose is to seek out other people they can argue with online. As the word suggests, they hide behind anonymous names and, as soon as they find a blogger who is willing to publish their comments and fight back, they tuck in and make themselves at home. If you scroll through any of the posts on my blog, you might think I'm one of the lucky few who doesn't have any trolls. That is a lie. In fact, I have many. I simply don't let their comments invade our space. I delete comments from trolls for the same reason Brené Brown doesn't read reviews: As she says, it doesn't serve the work. But unlike Brené Brown, in order to know which comments to delete, I have to read them first.

The opinions of me and my apartment varied among the trolls who stopped by that week. One person believed I had staged the pictures and hid my clutter behind the scenes in each one. Another felt my home was soulless and that I, in turn, was soulless. The majority seemed most concerned with my tiny wardrobe, however—specifically that it didn't seem like I had any appropriate outfits to wear on dates. "No wonder you got dumped last month," one comment said.

Replying with a fish-eye lens view of my apartment wouldn't have convinced the first person my photos weren't staged. Trying to explain that I felt more at home in my home now than ever before wouldn't have helped the second person sense the soul in the space. And taking pictures of myself in every outfit I owned that could be considered date-appropriate wouldn't have helped any of us. There hadn't been many comments from trolls that hurt before, but that one stung. The breakup with Andrew was too recent—and the sting got worse when a friend made a similar remark only days later.

She hadn't been in my life for long at the time, this friend. And she wasn't a particularly good friend, if the word *good* described someone I spent a lot of time with or entrusted with my deepest and darkest secrets. But she was a good enough friend that it hurt. After reading the same blog post the trolls had commented on, she called me to report that she could not believe how clean and organized my apartment was. "I'm seriously in shock!" she exclaimed. "Can you do my place next?" We talked about some of the most troublesome areas in her home. Her desk covered in paperwork, and projects she wanted to tackle but never had time for. Her front closet, which was filled with shoe boxes stacked on top of more shoe boxes. Shoes she had also spent good money on at one time, but now never wore or brought out only once a year. And her wardrobe. "My closet is literally stuffed. I wouldn't even know where to start," she said. Before I could laugh or make a suggestion or react in any way, she added one more thing. It was both her way of setting a personal boundary for how she would deal with her clutter and also a deep dig at mine. "But I don't want my closet to look like yours. You'll never meet a man with those outfits, girl!"

Now, here's the thing. It wasn't that her comment or the troll's comment struck a particular chord. I had always been someone who wore the same few outfits, and that had never affected my ability to date or to be seen as a person worth dating. And if I flipped that story, the same was also true for every guy I had dated. Whatever they wore (and I do mean whatever, because I can't for the life of me recall what any of my exes used to wear), it did not affect my opinion of them. But the comments took me back to a place I'd been many times before. A place where I felt the need to take a stand and make a point—but stopped myself short. I wanted to say, "I don't care what you wear, so why do you care what I wear?" Instead, I said nothing.

I had always said nothing.

When I was 24, I decided to stop eating meat and switch to a plant-based diet. It only lasted for four years before I went back to eating some meat, but I spent those four years feeling like I had to explain myself to everyone I dined with. The majority of the people in my life acted like my being a vegetarian was an inconvenience—as though the fact that I would not be putting the meat of a cow or pig or bird or fish into my mouth somehow affected their ability to eat with me. I walked into every barbecue dinner knowing I'd be asked if I wanted any carrots and hummus to go with my veggie burger, and that someone would likely shove a package of raw meat in my face and ask, "Don't you miss it?" I always knew how to laugh it off. But I also always wanted to say, "I don't care if you eat meat, so why do you care if I don't?" Instead, I said nothing.

The same was true when I decided to stop drinking. Unlike giving up meat, this is obviously a decision that has stuck. And because people can see how much happier and healthier I am—on all fronts, mind, body, and soul—almost nobody has questioned it. But there were still a few who did, and their comments cut deep. "You were so fun when you drank." *Was I the definition of boring now?* "I wish you would drink with us tonight, but no pressure!" *Sure, no pressure at all.* "That means we can never have drunk sex!" A guy I dated briefly said that last one, as though drunk sex had ever been an enjoyable experience. I've also been introduced at parties as "the sober one," and later been handed a glass of champagne for a toast and been told, "Just take a sip, it's not a big deal!" "Are you *really* never going to drink again?" was my least favorite question to answer, second only to the one I got when I was a vegetarian: "Don't you miss it?" Of course I missed it. You can't end a 14-year relationship with someone or something and expect it to never cross your mind again. "STOP ASKING!" I always wanted to scream at them. "I don't care if you drink, so why do you care if I don't?" Sometimes I managed to mouth a simple "no" and that was enough. But more often than not, I pressed my lips together and I said nothing.

I was naive when I started the shopping ban. I never could have imagined I would find myself in the same trenches I had been in when I gave up meat and alcohol. The social landscape of shopping seemed flatter, with fewer mountains to climb. *Why should anyone care if I get rid of my stuff or don't shop for anything new? This doesn't affect anyone but me.* Oh, how naive I was.

Aside from the friend who made fun of my teeny-tiny wardrobe, I had a friend who constantly tried to convince me to give up on the ban so we could go to the outlet malls. Twice I went to keep her company, but both times I felt like the only sober person at the party. When I traveled to Toronto for work, my co-workers asked how the shopping ban was going and looked at me like I was crazy. "Better you than me," they said, as I walked past their desks noticing that almost every single computer screen was open to an online shopping website. There were also friends who justified purchases I wasn't even seriously considering. They told me I "deserved" it. "You work so hard!" they said. "And you only live once!" I hated the acronym for that truism: YOLO. I'd watched too many friends swipe their credit cards and go deep into debt on that rationale. That and "treat yourself" were the two phrases I wished could be erased from the urban dictionary and forgotten forever. Yes, you only live once. And you should enjoy it. But not if it means breaking your budget or going into debt for it. There's nothing fun about debt, and there is certainly no acronym to change that. I knew that all too well.

In all of these situations, I never got mad at my friends. I couldn't even blame them for trying to get me to shop

with them or shop for myself or simply enjoy my money—
this was a behavior many people learned and exhibited
in all kinds of circumstances in their lives. In my own
life, I'd had friends who would hand me another drink
and encourage me to stay out all night. I'd had friends
who suggested we switch to drugs so we could stay awake
longer. I'd also had friends who would happily skip a workout and suggest we split a large pizza instead. Now I had
friends who tried to justify why I should buy things for
myself. What we were consuming was different, but the
scenarios were always the same. And I couldn't pretend
the roles had never been reversed.

I don't have any specific memories of this—probably
because I blocked them out, the same way you block out
anything you don't want to remember about your former
self—but I am sure there were times when I encouraged
friends to break their own rules and do bad things with
me. I *know* I did. I know because that's what addicts do. It's
also what people within the same circle of influence do.
Over the years, I had developed dozens of friendships—
but I had also compartmentalized them all. I had friends
I drank with, friends I did drugs with, friends I ate junk
food with, and friends I shopped with. It was rare for me
to invite the friends I drank with over to my place when I
knew another friend and I were going to binge on takeout.
Occasionally I smoked weed and ate junk food with the
same people, but that was as close as I came to combining
any of my worlds. And within each one of those worlds, I
know we were all guilty of influencing one another.

The problem, in my friends' eyes, was that I was the
first one to leave those worlds. I quit doing hard drugs
when I was 23, and I quit smoking weed when I was
25. *Good-bye, drug world. See you never again.* Then I quit

drinking when I was 27 and left that world behind too. I can't say I never eat bad food, but the healthier I got, the more self-aware I became about what I was putting into my body. I eventually stopped binging and stopped inviting friends to binge with me. And even though the three worlds were completely separate, after I left each one, the same list of comments started flooding in: first the jokes, then the justifications, the reminders of the good times, and the pleas to come back.

I didn't think anyone would care that I quit shopping, but I also never got mad at my friends when they started making comments that expressed otherwise, because I knew the truth, which was that I had left them too. I had broken the rules and rituals that had bound our friendship in the shopping world. We would no longer be able to find pleasure in buying things at the same time or talking about the deals we got or sharing tips on how to save. I had always known that drinking alcohol was deeply ingrained in our culture and was a main talking point at almost all events, but I had never even thought about the fact that shopping and spending money might've been an even bigger thing we bond over. See? Naive. So I couldn't get mad at my friends for feeling as though I'd just removed myself from what was probably one of the most common topics of discussion.

As time went on, I noticed more and more friends acted like they couldn't recap their own shopping ventures in front of me, the same way you wouldn't curse in front of a child. "Sorry, Cait, you won't care about this next story," they would say before sharing with the group. *Should I cover my ears? Or go sit in the corner?* Eventually, a few people stopped inviting me to anything that involved spending money at all. They seemed confused by the whole experiment, and assumed that because I couldn't shop, I also couldn't go out for dinner. Those assumptions hurt, because they made me feel like I was being ostracized for trying to better myself. Was this what it felt like to be one of the smart kids who actually cared about their education and their grades in high school? I wanted to reach out and tell my friends that just because I was changing didn't mean they had to. "I don't care that you still shop, so why do you care that I don't?" Instead, I said nothing. I always said nothing. But it did make me wonder, *Why do we encourage each other to spend money, when we should all be saving more?*

One lesson I've learned countless times over the years is that whenever you let go of something negative in your life, you make room for something positive. Releasing the toxic relationship with Chris that had once gripped me opened my eyes to the fact that I could, in fact, go back to school and pursue some of my dreams. Leaving my job in the public sector gave me the opportunity to see that I could write for a living. Even doing something as simple as choosing not to finish a book I didn't like gave me more time to read books I loved. And putting less energy into the friendships with people who didn't understand me gave me more energy to put into the friendships with people who did.

While a few friendships slowly faded out, I found many more grew and flourished throughout the shopping ban. I got together with Kasey, whom I had gone to Portland with, every couple of weeks. She was one of the few friends I knew I could always talk shop with (so to speak), as we both worked for financial startups and understood the struggles in doing so. But she was also one of the most positive people I had ever met. Her energy was infectious, and I needed to be infected with good energy. If we didn't go for brunch somewhere in Vancouver, we often went for a walk in Port Moody that almost always ended at Rocky Point Ice Cream. I also needed to be infected with a single scoop of salted caramel from time to time.

Tanya was another friend who infected me with her positive energy. She was the first friend I made when I moved to Port Moody, and the first person I would call anytime I wanted to go for a hike, because I knew she would always say yes. Every other weekend, we explored any one of the dozens of trails between Port Moody and Pitt Meadows. My favorite was always our three-hour strolls around Buntzen Lake with her dog, Starr. We were never in a hurry to get to the end, and it showed in both the stride of our steps and the pace of our conversation.

When I originally decided to do the shopping ban, though, the first person I shared the idea with was my best friend, Emma. Emma and I first met when we were working as deli clerks at a grocery store in Victoria. There was a three-year age gap between us: she was 17 at the time, and I was about to turn 20. But our goofy and often crude sense of humor was as similar as our matching beige-top-and-black-bottom uniforms. We'd only worked together for two years, but we had been inseparable ever since.

Emma was the first person I told everything to. She was the first person I told how much debt I had. She was the first person I sent the link of my blog to. She was the first person with whom I shared my decisions to start working out more and drink less and eventually quit drinking altogether. It didn't matter where I was in the world—living in Port Moody, working in Toronto, or traveling anywhere else—Emma has always been the first to know about anything in my life, and vice versa.

Over the years, I have come to believe there are two types of friends in this world: the friend who will save you from going home with the random person you met at the bar, and the friend who will celebrate your sexual escapade over Bloody Marys the next morning. The one who will never miss a scheduled date to go to the gym, and the one who will congratulate you for eating two cheeseburgers, an order of fries, and a milkshake after a bad day. The one who will stop you from spending $300 on a bag you don't need, and the one who will drive you to the nearest store to buy it. I also believe we choose who we share these internal struggles with before we make our final decisions, because we almost always tell the person who will enable us to make the bad choice. The reason Emma was the first person I told everything to was because she firmly fell into the camp of friends who encourage people to make good choices.

During the first few months of the ban, I shared with Emma every urge I had to shop. My text messages ran the gamut:

From rational: "I've been thinking about replacing my bedding."

To frantic: "Help! I'm one click away from buying it all! Stop me! Ahhh!"

To deflated: "This is the worrrrrrrst, why am I doing this!?!?!?!?!"

Emma's responses almost always started with a laugh. She is the kind of friend who can laugh at you without leaving you feeling judged, because you know that's not why she's laughing. We would both go into hysterics talking about how ridiculous some of my messages were, and especially some of the things I was thinking about breaking the ban for. It wasn't judgment—it was seriously funny. And when we were done laughing, Emma had the magical ability to put me in my place by repeating my own words back to me. She said things like:

"Is it on the approved shopping list? Are you willing to swap it out for something that is on the list?"

"Babe, you're fine! You didn't need it yesterday, so you don't need it today."

"You're doing amazing! One decision at a time! Just TCB!" (This was our code for: take care of business.)

She was my cheerleader and my champion for success. I have often attributed some of my ability to repay my debt so quickly to my readers who helped me stay account-able, and I still stand by that. But Emma was—and is—the ultimate accountability partner. That's not to say we always made the best decisions. In the first 10 years of our friendship, we occasionally let each other off the hook and made some of those bad choices. But we never judged each other, because we always knew we'd get back on track quickly—and if it took too long, we would step in to guide each other there.

Finally, there was Clare. Clare and I first met through our personal finance blogs. As I wrote about paying off my consumer debt, she wrote about paying off her student loans. Her writing was smart and quick-witted. There was a reason she became a copywriter. Clare was born to be a copywriter. She was also one of my only sober friends.

Before I actually quit drinking, I e-mailed the author of a sobriety blog written by a woman who used the pen name "B." In desperation, I shared my concerns and inse-curities with B. I bared my soul to a complete stranger. Only she wasn't a complete stranger. Within hours of hitting "Send," I checked my e-mail and found a short and sweet reply. "Babe, before I respond to everything you shared, I have to be honest. It's me, Clare. I am also B." The Internet had worked its magic—twice—to make sure we crossed paths, and we'd been friends ever since. She was my Sober Sally, and I hers. Clare's love and support was as fierce as her red hair. She always reminded me she was a "ride or die" friend. That she would stand by me through anything. And she did. But we didn't actually meet face-to-face for the first time until two years later, on the night before her wedding day in October 2014.

The best and worst part about building friendships with people you meet online is they almost never live in the same city as you. In this case, Clare lived in Denver. Being 1,500 miles apart made it difficult to get together for a casual coffee, but when she invited me to her wedding, I did not hesitate to RSVP. Of course, I was going. It would be an honor, and also, I just wanted to meet my Internet best friend in real life.

The original plan was for Andrew to come with me, but even without him I was determined to fit the trip into my budget, and I did. On top of the money I was investing in my retirement funds each month, I was also setting aside money for travel. I had spent almost my entire 20s talking about how I wanted to travel more and complaining that I never had the money to do it. Now, thanks to the shopping ban, I finally had the money. In fact, I had enough for my return flight, my hotel, and food, and even a rental car for four days. I used airline points and discount codes to make it cheaper, but still, I had the money for it all.

It was my second time in the Mile High City, but the first time I would be able to leave the downtown core and do something besides the conference activities that had brought me there before. Apart from the wedding, there was only one thing I wanted to do: spend a day in the mountains with my friend Kayla. Kayla was yet another personal finance blogger. We had met at a conference in St. Louis in 2013, and I immediately felt she would be one of my people. At this point, Kayla was the only other person I knew who wrote about both money and mindfulness. She was also the only friend who had experience with meditation, and with whom I could share some of my more "woo woo" thoughts.

After I woke up with the sun, Kayla picked me up from my hotel. We sipped coffee from the two travel mugs she'd brought, stopped for breakfast in Morrison, then drove to Red Rocks Park. It was here that I learned the importance of drinking twice as much water as you normally would, when you're nearly 6,500 feet above sea level. Climbing the stairs at the amphitheater, I was short of breath from the lack of oxygen. Standing between the two monoliths, my view came with a slight spin. But for someone who'd grown up in the Pacific Northwest, surrounded by the ocean and the Coast Mountains, the red sandstone was a vision. The 250-million-year-old layered rock formations greeted us around every corner of our hike back down to the car. There's a reason Red Rocks Amphitheatre was once considered one of the Seven Wonders of the Natural World, and I was grateful to see it.

Later that night, I drove with Clare and her soon-to-be husband, Drew, to a party their friends were throwing for them in Boulder. She didn't introduce me as the sober one, but as her Internet BFF. "Cait is an amazing writer, you have to read her blog," she shouted above the music. "She's writing about a yearlong shopping ban she's doing—it's incredible!" And with that, she left me to mingle, not stuck in the uncomfortable position of feeling like I was the only sober person at the party, but like I was a valued peer among friends.

At their wedding reception the next day, I met even more of Clare and Drew's friends, including another Sober Sally. We danced until our feet hurt and I knew it was time to go. Saying good-bye to Clare that night was short and sweet, as though we might actually be able to meet for that casual coffee the following week. I knew we wouldn't meet again that soon, but we would, in fact, meet again. The Internet had worked its magic—twice—to make sure we crossed paths and became friends. The shopping ban had worked its own magic and made sure we could meet in real life.

# 5

# november:
# blacking out and
# coming to

**months sober:** *22*
**income saved:** *30%*
**confidence I can complete this project:** *40%*

One of the things I've learned in the handful of years I've been blogging is that the readers who leave comments (aside from the trolls) are generally one of two types of people: those who are inspired by and support whatever you are doing, and those who think it's a nice idea but are quick to list every possible reason for why they couldn't do the same. Their partner doesn't want to give up drinking or dining out or shopping, their kids refuse to give away their belongings, they work too many hours each week to make extra money on the side, they have houses to maintain and friends to see and events to go to, and so on. These readers fill the tiny comment box with their stories, and share personal struggles with such intimate detail that I have often wondered if even their partners know it to be true. And if they are feeling particularly down, in that moment, they will close with two punctuation marks: a colon and a opening parenthesis—the digital sad face.

I have never, and will never, argue with the reasons my readers give for why they can't do what I am doing. I have always said that personal finance is personal, and what works for one person won't always work for another, and that's true of most everything. But there is one struggle my readers share that I can relate to. More than that, I've lived and wrestled with it many times.

It's the concern that banning yourself from doing something altogether will be too restrictive. That going cold turkey will cause you to eventually give up, relapse, and binge harder than you might have if you'd never attempted to abstain. Without question, this was the most common objection readers made when I started writing about my ban, and the most common reason they said doing one wasn't an option for them. To be fair, it's a valid concern—especially if you've ever thought shopping could solve a problem in your life. What I mean by that goes beyond the superficial terms of "retail therapy." It runs deeper than the shallow belief I could buy my way to happiness. It wasn't even the digs some of my friends made about the challenge itself that caused me to question my reason for wanting to complete it. It was what I said to myself, whenever I thought about giving up—because I did think about giving up. And one time, I actually did.

Back in July, I had taken extensive measures to make sure I would see as few advertisements as possible throughout the year. I had gotten rid of cable and hooked up my television so it could only stream Netflix, years before, so I wouldn't be exposed to ads on that screen. However, my eyes still had to scroll past them on my computer and on my phone. I couldn't control the ad placements on websites, but I could control some of what I saw on social media, so that's where I started. On each of the platforms I used (Facebook, Twitter, and Instagram), I reviewed the list of accounts I was following and unfollowed all the stores. There were bookstores, outdoors stores, home decor stores, and department stores. Aside from the bookstores, I wondered why I had followed some of these accounts to begin with. *Did I really need to know when picture frames or luggage sets or bathrobes went on sale? Had that ever been important?*

I tripped up over businesses my friends owned, like the line of natural beauty products that I had actually switched over to. *How could I unfollow Megan's accounts? Would unfollowing them make it seem like I didn't support her work? Would it seem like I didn't support* her? The simple fact that I was asking myself this question proved otherwise. Of course, I supported my friends' products and services—I just couldn't be tempted by them for the next year.

When I was done with social media, I tackled my in-box, which was a beast of its own. Fortunately, there was an application that could help with this, which pulled together a long list of the 300-plus newsletters I had apparently subscribed to over the years, and put a big red "unsubscribe" button next to each one. Again, there were bookstores, outdoors stores, home decor stores, and department stores. Unsubscribe, unsubscribe, unsubscribe, unsubscribe. But there were also airlines and travel deal websites that notified me about discount codes and flash sales. I struggled with the decision to remove these future e-mails from my life. *I am allowed to spend money on travel this year. Shouldn't I try to save money whenever I book a trip? I am a personal finance blogger, after all! I can't tell people I spent more when I could have spent less.* Even though the sentiment was valid, I knew hearing about more deals would only cause me to spend more money. In a matter of minutes, I had unsubscribed from them all—or so I thought. Somehow, despite all the measures I had taken, one e-mail slipped through the cracks and appeared in my in-box on Black Friday.

It started as a morning like any other. Shower, make coffee, read a book, then start work. It was slow and quiet. I wasn't preoccupied with thoughts of clutter. I didn't crave my former routine of buying take-out coffee. And I didn't clue in to the fact that it was Black Friday until I checked my e-mail and saw one from my favorite retailer with sale prices splashed across the screen. Buy-one-get-one deals, a 25-percent-off book button, a 40-percent-off book button, and 50 to 75 percent discounts on candles. Red letters for all of it that were big and bold and in my face. Before I could click the button that would send the e-mail to my spam folder, I noticed e-readers were $40 off the regular price—from $139 marked down to just $99. This was perfect. I had committed to giving away an e-reader on my blog the week before, but had yet to buy one. For once, my procrastination had (literally) paid off.

And then I heard it.

*You've never seen e-readers priced that low before.*

I knew the voice well. It was familiar, like when you answer the phone and hear a friend you haven't spoken to in years on the other end, and you're filled with love and excitement to talk to her again. There was an immediate recognition of the level of comfort between us that allowed me to take some of my walls down and let her words come in.

*You've never seen e-readers priced that low before. And you need this.*

We had history, the voice and I. In fact, I've had more conversations with her than with anyone else. She knew me on a molecular level—what it took to feed me, fuel me, make me come alive—and what it took to crush me. I had always trusted that she would help me solve any problem. After all, my own existing e-reader was broken. I did need this, didn't I?

*You need this. And you haven't bought anything for yourself in so long.*

She had also always been my sounding board. Whenever I stood at a crossroads and didn't know which route to take, she considered both options with me. This time, we were at the most famous junction in the personal finance world and it asked only one question: Do you have the money? I knew the answer, but I still looked to her for guidance.

*You need this. You haven't bought anything for yourself in so long. And you have the money!*

My eyes grew wide and I felt a little dance move up from my chest and into my shoulders. It was the same feeling I used to get when I picked up two bottles of wine and knew a fun night was ahead of me—a mix of excitement and anxiety, chased with a shot of adrenaline. I had $700 in my shopping ban account. Of course I could afford this! I was ready to flirt with the idea, make a move, and dance all night. Only, I wasn't the same girl who picked up two bottles of wine anymore, so the feeling now made me pause.

She could tell I wasn't convinced.

*And it may never be $40 off again.*

That was all I needed to hear, and she knew it. She knew it, because I knew it.

I don't specifically remember what happened next, but I know the order in which it must have taken place. I would've had to add two e-readers to the shopping cart, enter my credit card and shipping information, review the order, and hit "Submit." I know that had to have taken place, because that's what I had done hundreds of times before. It was as familiar to me as getting dressed each morning, or finding the part in my hair, which is to say it came naturally. It wasn't just a habit, it was part of me. But I don't remember doing it. I don't remember entering any information or clicking any buttons. The next thing I knew, there was another e-mail from my favorite store— this one confirming my order. I had lost all the seconds in between to yet another blackout and, in that time, I had broken the shopping ban.

I was no stranger to what could come next. I knew how quickly a small slip could turn into a downward tumble and a full-on relapse, because that also seemed to come naturally to me. Like the time I tried the diet where I had to restrict myself to 1,200 calories a day. It lasted all of four days before I convinced myself I could handle one piece of dark chocolate. But the one piece of dark chocolate quickly turned into the entire bar of dark chocolate. And who the heck was I kidding? *I couldn't do this stupid diet, so why stop there?* I got into my car and drove to the grocery store to buy a frozen pizza and a slice of chocolate cheesecake, because that was what I had really wanted all along—not the piece of dark chocolate. *Diets are dumb,* I told myself. *I'm never doing that again.* Then I brought the real food home and promptly ate it all in one sitting. Only I don't remember eating it all in one sitting. One minute it was in my basket at the grocery store, and the next minute there were two plates on the coffee table in front of me containing one fork and a few crumbs. The cardboard pizza box, plastic container, and receipt were the only proof of what I had put into my body during the minutes in between.

I'd had a lot of food blackouts over the years. When I was a kid, I used to sneak into the kitchen at night when everyone was asleep, steal the package of cookies from the cupboard, and bring it back to bed with me. I wanted to eat one or two cookies—that was all. But before I knew it, I was hiding the empty package at the bottom of the garbage can, hoping no one would realize what I had done. If I dug deep enough so even I couldn't see it, maybe I could forget about what I had done too. Halloween candy was the worst. If my parents dared to buy any too early, I made sure it was gone, and they would have to buy more before the big day. And I could never understand how it was possible my friends were still bringing pieces of it in their lunches in mid- to late November, when mine had only lasted a few days. If I had it, I ate it. End of story.

In 2012, my second-to-last attempt at quitting drinking turned into the ultimate slip-up and relapse. I was sober for all of 45 days before I decided enough was enough. I was tired of telling people I wasn't drinking at events, and sick of the responses I got when I tried to string together words that explained why. I only had two beers that night, but I then felt it was my duty to drink everything in sight for the next six weeks, to make up for the six weeks I had just wasted being sober. I don't remember all the drinks I had or all the things I did while I was drunk. None of it mattered. I was simply done abstaining. Anything that got in my path was at risk of being consumed.

So, yes, I knew how quickly a small slip could turn into a full-on relapse. I also knew the biggest problem wasn't always the relapse itself, but the things I told myself about the relapse. I looked at myself in the mirror, grabbed my stomach, and cursed myself to be fat forever. *The cellulite isn't going anywhere, so why did you even bother?* Or I woke up and gave myself a verbal beating while looking at the physical bruises on my body—a reminder of how reckless I had been the night before. *Good job, Cait. You probably fell on your face in front of everyone yet again, like the train wreck you are.* Then there were the mornings I woke up fully dressed in bed with a pizza box on the floor, or sometimes even in bed with me—proof I had finished a night of binge drinking with a night of binge eating. I said the cruelest things of all to myself in the first few hours of those days.

But perhaps the worst was when I found out I had said or done something during a relapse that didn't align with my morals or my values, like lie about where I was or who I was with or what I was doing. *Why do my friends still talk to me?* I would ask myself. *I am a terrible person.* I didn't just feel guilty, I was deeply ashamed of my actions. In her second TED Talk, "Listening to Shame," Brené Brown says the difference is that guilt equals *I did something bad*, and shame equals *I am bad*. I was a permanent resident of the world of shame. I told myself I was a failure, and the attempt to improve myself wasn't successful, so I should just accept the fact that I was a failure and keep on failing. The same voice that had encouraged me to make the positive change was the voice that also talked me into going back to my old ways and the voice that later shamed me for it. Yet, because I knew the sound of that voice so well, I had always trusted her. I believed whatever she said and did whatever she told me. And then I took her beating afterward, because I felt I deserved that too. This is how and why the cycle of abuse and self-loathing continued for so many years. I always trusted her, because she was me.

Only now, as I looked at the order confirmation in my in-box, I knew I didn't want to be her anymore. And I really didn't want to let this slip turn into a relapse.

It had been a long time since I'd made a blackout purchase. Some people call them impulse purchases, but for me they truly felt like blackouts. Like I had slipped into a coma for 60 seconds and woken up with amnesia and a receipt. Surprisingly, when the confirmation e-mail appeared in my in-box this time, a new voice popped into my head. She didn't sound like anyone I'd heard before. Aside from being a little panicked, she was cheerful and encouraging.

*You don't need a new e-reader! Yours is perfectly fine! So what if you have to stick a pin in the reset button to turn it on? It works fine otherwise! It doesn't need to be replaced right now.*

She closed with some advice I'd never been given: *See if you can cancel the order!*

This was a different kind of impulse for me—one that would help me save money versus spend it, and find joy in what I had rather than assume I could buy more happiness. I was nervous it wouldn't work. I think it was the first time in my life I had attempted to cancel an order, and the thought that it might not be possible to do so doubled my heart rate. But it was possible, and I did cancel it—or rather, I removed one e-reader from the order and still bought the one I was giving away on my blog. Then I let out a sigh of relief so loud I swore my neighbors could have heard it through the concrete walls. If they had, their imaginations would've run wild with theories, never once guessing I had simply stopped myself from wasting money on something I didn't need.

As grateful as I was to have been able to remedy my mistake, I still spent the next two weeks wondering if I had failed. Occasionally, the old voice paid me a visit. She came with only one purpose, which was to try and shame me for what I had done. And she was right, to some extent. I had broken the shopping ban, momentarily, after all. It did feel like I had failed. I'd survived almost five months without making any unnecessary purchases. *Why had I talked myself into breaking the rules now? I was 162 days into the ban. Shouldn't I have been cured?*

I could've let the shame set in, felt like a failure, and given up on the shopping ban altogether. But slipping up didn't make me a bad person. I was not bad. What I did wasn't bad. I had just slipped up. And I knew I didn't want to relapse and repeat the cycle of self-loathing. It always led to trouble. The only way to stop it would be to remove the thing shame feeds on: secrecy. No one ever knew how bad I felt about all the things I'd talked myself into doing. I had to give this mistake its own voice. I had to be honest and admit to readers what I had done.

In a blog post titled "The Toughest Bad Habit to Kick," I shared the e-reader story, and talked about how I was learning that one of my worst habits was talking myself into doing things I knew I shouldn't do. And it was true. The tougher habit to kick, though, was learning not to shame myself for it. Realizing that making an error in judgment didn't make me a bad person. Getting comfortable with being human. The voice tried to talk me out of hitting "Publish." *Are you really going to admit to the world that you failed? That you're weak?* But there was nothing weak about it. The fact that I was able to see what I had done, know the action didn't align with what I wanted, and change my reaction showed how much progress I had made. It was a challenge, and a learning experience on how to practice living intentionally with a goal in mind. I wanted to become a more mindful consumer. I knew I didn't need a new e-reader. To buy one would have been to act on impulse, and there was nothing mindful about that.

There were always going to be outside influences at play. Advertisements and commercials weren't going to disappear. I couldn't avoid shopping malls or online stores forever. No matter how many accounts I unfollowed, I would always see things on social media. Even the clothing or backpacking gear that was in my friends' pictures had the potential to influence me, as did the listicles everyone published on their blogs of which books I should read each season. And people would always make comments. They would always make little digs at my intentions that would try to put cracks in the tiny bit of willpower I was still standing on, because people will always make comments when you decide to live a countercultural lifestyle. I couldn't avoid it, the same way I couldn't avoid anything else that could cause me to think about spending money. There were always going to be outside influences at play. But I could change my reactions to them—and that change had to start within.

6

# december: crafting new traditions

**months sober:** *23*
**income saved:** *10% (traveled all month again)*
**total number of belongings tossed:** *54%*

A few days after Black Friday, I hopped on yet another plane and flew to Toronto for work.

Work had started to become something of a sore spot for me. When I'd first started with the company more than two years before, we were a small team of six. We worked out of the CEO's living room, which was a shock to the system on my first day. *I had quit my job with the government to move across the country and work in someone's house? And use my own computer? Was this real life?* But the shock quickly wore off when I realized being at a company this small meant I could physically see my efforts pay off. When I was working for the government, I had struggled with the slow pace, and also with the understanding that I might never know who actually cared about the work I had done. Here, we crossed tangible things off our to-do lists every single day, and each one of them was important. We could track the numbers and analyze the data and see that our work mattered. It felt good, and it was exciting.

Every day looked different back then, which I also loved. Some days, I wore my editor hat and wrote content strategies and tackled writing projects. Other days, I wrote copy for infographics and worked with freelance graphic designers to bring them to life. And on other days still, I mapped out large-scale projects that would require the help of multiple freelance writers, so I hired them, delegated tasks, and published hundreds of pieces of content.

The most memorable moments, however, were the days we would swap hats. If our office manager was away, we had to go shopping for office supplies and toilet paper. We all answered the phone and helped users navigate the website, which proved to either be the most frustrating or the most entertaining part of the day. And if the CEO was late getting to the office for a meeting, we entertained the guests who arrived first. The best was witnessing their reactions when they realized we worked out of someone's home. There was no shame on our part anymore. We were the very definition of an early startup. It didn't matter where we worked, because our work mattered.

When I left Toronto to move back to B.C. and work from home, we were still a small team. There were five people in the office, and three more of us who worked remotely. Now, two years later, our team had grown to nearly 20 people—and most of them had joined us in the last six months. The remote workers were outnumbered by on-site workers, at this point, with one of us for every four of them. And by "us" I mean myself and a handful of developers. I don't think the developers minded being among the few remote workers, or even noticed, for that matter. It was in their nature to work alone, and I'm sure they were grateful for the ability to do so without interruption.

I, on the other hand, felt more and more disconnected from the team as it continued to grow. I didn't know many of the new people, and the distance made it nearly impossible to build real relationships with them. In my best attempt, I sent friendly e-mails and asked questions and set up meetings so we could talk further. But when we finally did talk further, I learned that more meetings happened without me now, simply because of the proximity the rest of the team had to one another. If you could lean across your desk to ask a question and make an executive decision, why wouldn't you? I knew it made sense, but it still hurt to be left out of those decisions—especially when they were about my projects.

There were other issues, of course. The work itself was no longer as fulfilling as it had once been, and I found myself dreading having to write yet another article for the sole purpose of having it rank high in Google. I had also started to miss the little things, like updates on the personal lives of the core six. We had been a family, at one point. We had spent 50 hours or more each week in a living room, with actual couches and a fireplace. Office space or not, this was the room where people put their feet up and shared stories—and we did just that. In November, we put up a Christmas tree, built a fire, and listened to Christmas music while we worked. It was our little home away from home, and I missed it. Now the team was working out of an office on King Street East, which was a huge step up for the company as a whole, and something they needed. But I wasn't part of it. Walking into the new space with its white walls and white furniture was exciting for them, but I always felt like I was invading it when I went to visit. Like there was no room for me there anymore. This trip did nothing to change that. It only made it worse.

The purpose of the trip was to attend our staff Christmas party. Our first Christmas party had taken place during my final six-week binge before I quit drinking in 2012, which should indicate that I was not on my best behavior. That was the same night I apparently changed outfits three times, eventually decided being in a dress was the best choice, and then left my jeans behind at the bar. But I was always a happy drunk, so I woke up to text messages from my co-workers saying how "cute" and "fun" and "funny" I had been the night before. I was good at drinking and I was good at partying. I hated that I had blacked out parts of that night, but their text messages validated my blackout by reminding me that I was good at this.

I'd flown back for our second Christmas party in 2013, which was also the first party I'd been to since I had quit drinking. I bought a new turquoise dress and a pair of black patent leather heels for the occasion. *This is what 28-year-old women should wear at parties*, I thought when I tried the dress on at the store. When I walked into the party, however, I suddenly felt like I was the only person pretending to be a grown-up in a room of actual grown-ups. Everyone was drinking and laughing and falling over, and yet still looked beautifully put together. I wasn't drinking and I didn't feel at all like myself in that outfit. I knew then that I did not fit in here anymore. I spent the majority of that party hanging out in the kitchen with a few friends, looking over their shoulders and feeling jealous about how much fun everyone else was having without me.

Two years into my sobriety, however, attending my second sober Christmas party felt better. Now on this trip, I wasn't exactly thrilled about the idea of being the only sober person in the room, but I was excited to spend time with everyone, especially the core six. I tried to mingle with some of the new members of the team, but it was not my strong suit anymore. Nobody was going to text me the next morning to say I was cute or fun or funny. Still, I tried. I did want to get to know them. At various points in the conversations, a few people mentioned that they read my blog. One of the new girls even said she'd been reading it for years. She confided in me that she had been inspired to start her own shopping ban for six months, listed the few things she was allowed to buy in that time, and shared the financial progress she had already made. We went on to talk about some of the things we used to waste money on, and what we were learning while decluttering at the same time. We had to yell most of this to each other over the music, but it felt so good to connect with someone on these topics—especially because I had felt disconnected from the team for so many months.

A few of us moved the conversation to the line for the bar. One of the stakeholders in our company was bartending for us. He was tall and successful and friendly, but had enough authority that I had always been a little bit intimidated by him. I mean, he was one of the reasons I had a job. He was one of the people who paid me, and agreed to pay me more every year, and even to let me move back to B.C. and continue to work from there. I respected him. When it was my turn, I stepped forward and he asked what he could get me. "Cait doesn't drink anymore!" one of my co-workers yelled out, at the same time I asked for one of the Sanpellegrino Limonatas I saw hiding behind the Diet Coke. He didn't seem to care that I didn't drink. He didn't care what I ordered. He reached for the can and asked if I wanted a glass with some ice, and that was the end of the conversation.

He didn't care. But I cared.

When people announce your sobriety, it can feel like they have taken the card you hold closest to your chest and revealed your darkest secret to the world, which is that you are weak. You might as well write "I can't handle my liquor" on the newly sober person's forehead, or a simpler "waste case" would do the trick. In situations like this party, it also makes you feel like they have whittled down your worth to one sentence and turned you into nothing more than office gossip. And few people ask for permission to do this, by the way. For some reason, many people are as comfortable announcing your sobriety as they are announcing what they had for lunch. What they might not realize is that one is a choice and the other is a survival tactic.

I wish I could say that, two years in, I was comfortable enough in my sobriety that I could laugh these moments off or use quick wit to change the topic, but I wasn't there yet. My co-worker's announcement hurt my feelings, and served as a reminder that that was all I was ever going to be to her: a novelty; something to talk about. I didn't want to be known as the sober one anymore. I wasn't just the sober one. There was more to me than that. Wasn't there?

I left the party early that night, and woke up the next morning anxious to get to the airport. I wanted to go home.

As soon as I landed in Vancouver, I picked up my car from the long-term parking lot and drove straight to the ferry terminal. It typically took four hours to get back to my hometown, including a long wait at the terminal, a 95-minute ride on the ferry, and another 30 minutes' drive to my parents' house. Because it's so time-consuming, most locals dread having to take the ferry, but I never minded. I usually spent the entire time in my car, reading a book, watching a movie on my laptop, or sleeping. If I had to guess, I would say I've spent at least 50 hours of my life sleeping on B.C. ferries.

I had decided to spend the rest of December in Victoria. No one there questioned my sobriety or the shopping ban or any of the other challenges I took on. They supported me and celebrated all the changes I made in my life—especially my family.

I know some people can't imagine spending two weeks in the tiny guest room in their parents' house over the holidays. After spending time with my friends' families and exes' families over the years, I had figured out that our family being as close as we were wasn't exactly common. It was special, and I had taken it for granted when I was a kid, but now I treasured it. Alli was still living at home while going to the University of Victoria, and Ben would be coming home for two weeks during his break from the University of Alberta. We would all be under one roof again for the holidays, and I couldn't imagine a better way to end the year.

I was especially eager to see what Christmas would look like for us in the year of my shopping ban. Growing up, though I had never been particularly religious, religion had always been in my life. All three of us had gone to church-run day care centers when we were kids. We attended an Anglican church for a while, shortly after my mom met my dad, whose family was from England. Most of my friends went to a Christian church up the street from our house, and I joined them on Sunday mornings if I had slept over the night before. And for the first few years of high school, a group of friends and I went to that same Christian church every Thursday night for youth group.

Still, I never felt attached to any one religion. I thought the ceremonies and traditions were beautiful, the sermons deep and meaningful, and the hymns made me want to sing as loud as I could so everyone could hear me. But no religion has ever spoken directly to me, or made me feel comfortable nodding in agreement to its list of beliefs. I won't put words in my family's mouths, but I believe the same could be said for most of us, based on the way we were raised and the role religion played—and did not play—in our lives. So Christmas, for us, was not a religious holiday. But yes, there were gifts. Oh, were there ever gifts.

The first Christmas I can remember was at the age of four. My mom, my aunt, and I had flown from Victoria to Windsor, Ontario, to visit my grandma and our extended family. At the time, I was still an only child, and the only grandchild my grandma had. Needless to say, I was spoiled. I woke up on Christmas morning to find her entire living room filled with gifts.

Christmases looked similar for the rest of my childhood, especially when our family grew from one kid to three. Presents poured out from under the tree and were stacked on coffee tables and side tables and even in other corners of the living room. This was the decade when advertising kicked up a notch, credit cards gained popularity, and consumerism started to run rampant. People wanted bigger homes, better cars, the latest trends, and more of everything. Even Madonna sang about how we lived in a material world. So it doesn't surprise me that this is what our Christmases turned into, nor do I think my parents meant to teach us that this was the meaning of the holidays. Instead, I feel bad that they got sucked into it. I feel bad that they spent their hard-earned dollars on things we probably didn't need. Scratch that—things we definitely didn't need. It was not uncommon for us to find items in the backs of our closets in the spring or summer that had been there since December 26.

Fortunately, as we got older, this tradition of filling the living room with gifts slowly petered out. My mom gave up on the idea that she had to spend the same amount of money on each of us, and make sure we each had the same number of gifts to open on Christmas morning. We only asked for a few things we needed and wanted, and the day became less about the gifts and more about the time we spent together. And even though my shopping ban rules allowed me to buy gifts for people during this year, the ban itself prompted some important conversations in our family.

In the early months of the shopping ban, I will admit, I thought I would have a list of things to ask for by the time Christmas rolled around. Surely, I would need some new clothes or want a handful of books. Instead, the exact opposite was true and there was only one thing I actually needed: a new pair of shoes. When my mom asked Alli and Ben what they wanted, their responses were similar. Even as university students, they both agreed there was nothing they really needed. We had all gotten to the stage where we could buy what we wanted for ourselves, and didn't feel good about simply passing money back and forth through cash or gift cards.

With this in mind, my mom and I first came up with the idea of exchanging no gifts at all this year. But not everyone was so quick to jump on board. My grandma, in particular, could not stomach the thought of giving her grandchildren nothing for Christmas. She didn't want to go overboard, but she did want to give us something. It was tradition, she said, and she wasn't wrong. It had been a tradition for the first 28 years of my life, and for all the years she had been on this earth. Traditions are the roots of families, a part of how we identify as members of the tribe. The thought of ripping them up from the ground was like wiping the slate clean and asking everyone to plant new seeds and start again. Of course the idea would be met with some resistance.

In the end, we compromised. Rather than all of us spending our usual hundreds and even thousands of dollars on gifts, we pooled $700 to be spent on seven of us (the five of us plus my aunt and grandma). The rules for what we could spend the money on were simple: We could only ask for things we truly needed and each person could have no more than $100 spent on them.

The shopping process was painless, as we had removed the added stress of having to wander through busy malls and guess what people wanted. When we woke up on Christmas morning, the living room looked almost exactly the same as it had the night before, now with only a few gifts under the tree and our stockings hung half-full. Every other year, we had rushed into the living room to open presents and then gone about the rest of our day. On this morning, we made and ate breakfast as a family first, then spent a few minutes opening our gifts, and giving bigger hugs and more meaningful thank-yous than ever before.

When we were done, we packed up our two Yorkshire terriers, Molly and Lexie, and drove down to Willows Beach. The weather was perfect for a walk, with the warm sun beaming down on us and the air just cold enough that you could see your breath. "The girls," as we called them, raced up and down the sand with all the other dogs, whose owners we exchanged merry greetings with. Then Alli set up her camera and tripod, and we took family photos for the very first time. I repeat, the very first time. We had taken family photos when it was my mom, my dad, and I. We had taken more when Alli was born. But when Ben was born, and during all the years in between, we had never once all stood in front of a camera and asked someone to take pictures of us. These pictures on the beach didn't come out perfect. There was a little too much light behind us, so our faces appeared darker than they were. The girls wiggled to escape from my dad's arms. And the angle somehow made Alli look taller than me, even though I am, in fact, five inches taller than she is. But they captured the best Christmas we've ever had. They also captured the last Christmas we would ever spend together.

# 7

# january:
# rewriting
# the rules

**months sober:** *24*
**income saved:** *56%*
**confidence I can complete this project:** *90%*

I returned to my apartment in Port Moody on New Year's Eve, and invited Kasey over to celebrate the occasion. We put together a couple plates of cheese, crackers, vegetables, and desserts, drank sparkling water, and watched holiday movies in front of my fireplace. I know I can speak on Kasey's behalf when I say we also happily parted ways around 10 o'clock and were both asleep before midnight. These days, it was everything I hoped for in a party.

January was shaping up to be a quiet month. I only had one trip planned: five days in Toronto for work again. This would give me a chance to not only spend more time at home, but also save more money. I was happy with the progress I'd made in the first half of the shopping ban— saving an average of 19 percent of my income. Compared to the 10 percent or less (because I have to be honest and say it was usually less) I'd been saving every month before, this felt good. But I still knew I could do better. Whenever I went to Toronto for work, my only expense was food and entertainment—things I did with friends during the hours I wasn't at the office. In the middle of January, most people hibernated in their homes during those hours, in an attempt to escape the cold winds that blew through the streets of the cement jungle. This meant I would spend the majority of my off-time on this trip curled up on my old roommate's couch with her dog, Charlie. My heart and my wallet were ready for it.

When I arrived at Jen's apartment, I walked into a scene all too familiar. There were black garbage bags everywhere. One next to another next to another, against the wall in her hallway leading from the front door to the living room. At the top of the stairs, there were more bags leading to the bedrooms, as well as plastic tote containers and cardboard boxes. I didn't know what was inside, but I knew *exactly* what was inside: stuff Jen had decided she no longer wanted in her two-story apartment. She was decluttering.

Jen and I had grown up together in Victoria. Our parents lived only a few blocks from each other, so we'd gone to school together since third grade, when my family first moved to that neighborhood. We had sleepovers and played night league basketball, as kids. Our interests took us down different paths in high school, but we found our way back to each other in college and had been close ever since. I visited her in Toronto, shortly after my breakup with Chris in 2008, and knew it was a city I wanted to spend more time in. When I started working for the financial startup in 2012, Jen invited me to move into the guest bedroom in her rent-controlled apartment. Now she let me stay with her whenever I came into town. Jen's home felt like my home, and she was more like a sister than a friend.

It wasn't until I found myself standing among the bags and boxes of clutter, however, that I looked at everything Jen was choosing to keep and started to see who she really was. There were paintings she had done in frames she sanded down and refinished herself. Tables and sideboards she had done the same to, some of which housed drawers she had lined with wallpaper or painted bold colors. Prints and photo albums she had created to document some of her most memorable vacations with friends. The giant clock that had 12 antique cups and saucers glued to it, one for each hour it had to tick by. And her chalkboard wall that was always covered in new quotes and drawings. *How had I never noticed how creative Jen was? How talented and inventive and expressive she was? In 20 years of knowing each other and even living together, how had I never seen this before?*

I took this thought back home with me and began to wonder why I had never been more creative in my own life. It certainly wasn't for the lack of creativity and talent in my family. When my mom was young, she could always be found with a guitar in her hands. She even applied and was accepted to study music in college, but decided not to go, and instead moved to Toronto and later Vancouver and then Victoria. But her guitar went with her, and she could always be found with it in her hands. I remember listening to her play and sing when I was a kid. My mom loved rock and roll, and if she wasn't playing, we were listening to bands like Aerosmith, Guns N' Roses, Led Zeppelin, Pearl Jam, Pink Floyd, and the Tragically Hip. When she wasn't in the room, I sometimes opened the guitar case and strummed the strings, just to see what making music felt like.

My mom was someone who always kept her hands busy. When I was born, she and my aunt were leasing a retail space on Lower Johnson Street in Victoria, which is now home to one of the most hipster clothing stores in the city. There, they sold fabric by the yard next to things they had designed and made with it. Children's clothes, T-shirts, leggings, and dresses draped over hangers. My aunt also quilted, and they sold the quilts she made there too. It seems to me now that my mom never stepped away from her sewing machine for long. What clothing she couldn't find for me at thrift stores, she made for me instead—including the most elaborate Halloween costumes a kid could ask for. When I was four, she turned me into Minnie Mouse, with the gloves, shoes, ears, and bow. At eight, I was a blonde-haired Princess Jasmine from the popular movie *Aladdin*. Costumes seemed to be her specialty, as she went on to do all of the same for Alli, including designing her figure skating skirts and competition dresses. She turned that last one into a small business and quickly became the most sought-after dressmaker in the figure skating club.

My dad was the same, albeit his creativity came in the more constructive form. The house we grew up in was the same one he had grown up in, sold to him and my mom when his mom retired and moved to Wales, and his hand-iwork could be seen in every room. You could still see faint lines in the basement ceiling, from when he helped his dad tear down walls and create an open-concept space. He converted the garage into a fully functioning kitchen when my grandma first moved out from Ontario and lived with us for a while. When his own mom passed away, he used his inheritance to build a 900-square-foot garage with his own two hands. He cut back the square footage of the deck that was attached to the house, then eventually removed it altogether and poured a new cement patio in the backyard. When the exterior drain tile system needed to be replaced, he dug a trench around the entire house and did the job himself. He also ripped off the stucco, cut and painted and put up new siding, replaced all the win-dows, and installed two wood stoves. My dad was a bit impulsive. As soon as he saw a problem, he figured out how to fix it and started the work—and did everything to code, no less. The difference between us was that he actually solved the problem. I just purchased things with the intention to solve it one day, and one day didn't come very often.

Together, it's not surprising my parents combined their individual strengths and came up with even more creative solutions for around the house—namely for what was brought into the kitchen. My dad built garden beds the size of queen mattresses, and we filled them with veg-etables of all different shapes, colors, and sizes. Squash, zucchini, cucumbers, potatoes, turnips, carrots, tomatoes, and herbs. I can still remember running out to the beds with a pair of scissors, sinking my toes into the soil, and cutting chives to go with our dinner. The right side of the yard was lined with a row of fruit trees. From the back:

apple, pear, plum, three cherries—and peaches and nectarines squeezed in at the end, right up against the house. On the left side of the yard, more apple trees plus overgrown blackberry and loganberry bushes that poured over from the neighbors'. In the spring, we spent our weekends picking and canning fruit—no small feat in our tiny kitchen where we were constantly squeezing around each other. When summer turned to fall, we made homemade blackberry jam (still my favorite), and baked and froze enough apple, blueberry, and blackberry pies to get us through Christmas. My dad made the crusts and my mom made the filling. It was always a team effort.

My parents took pride in being able to do everything themselves. Why had I not done the same? Why hadn't I taken more of an interest and been more creative and adopted their skills? And why hadn't I appreciated everything they had done together for us? These questions were pressing enough on their own. They turned into an obsession when Alli called to tell me she thought our parents were getting a divorce.

I never predicted a day would come when I would hear my sister say those words: "I think Mom and Dad are going to get divorced."

Some kids see it coming. They grow up having to listen to their parents fight and live in a house full of tension. Some kids might even know it's so bad they almost pray for the end to be near. That was not the house we were raised in. I never predicted a day would come when I would hear my sister say those words.

She called me crying—sobbing so hard, I kept having to remind her to breathe. I begged her to calm down and explain, but her words made no sense. Between gasps for air, she told me she didn't have any proof, it was just a feeling. She had overheard a few strange conversations, and saw little signs pop up all over the house that put the idea in her head, but she had no proof. Still, she could not be convinced otherwise.

I couldn't put any of the pieces together for her. In December, my mom had asked if I would come back to Victoria and take care of the dogs in February, if she and my dad booked a trip to Cuba. They were looking at dates and just needed to confirm my dad's work schedule, but they would make a decision soon. That conversation had taken place only three weeks earlier, after the best Christmas we'd ever had. How could things have changed so drastically since? It was impossible. Alli couldn't have been right.

I asked her to keep me posted on any updates and told her she could call me anytime. She did, and she was right—things seemed off. Being a ferry ride away, all I could do was touch base with everyone more often and see what I could gather from our conversations. My mom seemed happy to hear from me at first, but then grew distant. My dad was uncharacteristically quiet. The man who had something to say about everything all of a sudden didn't have much to say about anything at all. We went from being a family that talked about everything to a family that talked about the weather.

Alli went through a phase where she thought the problem was her. She would call to ask if I thought things would get better if she started doing more to help around the house or getting better grades in school. Again, I begged her to calm down and told her she could do whatever she thought would help her feel better, but that it was not her fault. Whatever was going on between our parents was not her fault. I didn't know much, but I knew that was true.

I didn't tell Alli about some of the questions I was asking myself. That's the curse of being the eldest, especially by eight and ten years: you have to carry the weight of your younger siblings' problems, as well as your own. They come to you for a reason. You don't want to shelter them, but you do want to protect them. You want to protect them from the confusion and the pain, so you carry theirs and yours. Only, nobody knows you have your own confusion and pain. Nobody knows you're hurting at all.

I didn't wonder if I was part of the problem—not to say I'd been perfect or my parents had never fought about how to deal with my antics when I was younger, but I was a grown-up now. We all were. There was no way Alli, Ben, or I were part of the problem. However, I did ask myself what I could do to fix it. Even if it was just a patch job for now, I would do it. We, as a family, were lost, and I would do anything to get everyone back on the boat and steer us in the right direction.

This was the role I had always played in our family. With my dad being gone half the year, I grew up knowing I had to be ready to roll up my sleeves and help whenever it was needed. Alli and Ben didn't have the same responsibilities. They were asked to wash the dishes and take out the garbage. I was asked to take care of them. I wasn't one of "the kids"—I was the third adult. I had always been fine with it. I thought I was fine with it. But imagining my parents splitting up brought me back to reality, which was that I was one of their kids and I didn't want this to happen. I wanted my family to stay together.

The further I felt like things were slipping from my grasp, the more I started asking myself why I hadn't appreciated everything my parents had done together for us. Why hadn't I let my mom teach me how to sew? Flashbacks of asking her to help with—no, making her do—my sewing projects in high school filled me with regret. Why hadn't I at least watched what she was doing? Shown some interest in her interests? Even considered learning a skill that might actually help me? And why hadn't I let my dad teach me how to change the oil in my car? Why hadn't I at least watched what he was doing? Shown some interest in his interests? Even considered learning a skill that might actually help me? What had I done instead?

I knew the answer to that last question, which was that I paid for things. At some point, between growing up in the digital revolution, being part of what I liked to call the "Pinterest generation" (where everyone likes things to be new and matching), and moving out on my own, I had opted not to learn any of the same skills my parents had, knowing I could pay—and cheap prices, at that—for everything instead. I valued convenience over the experience of doing anything for myself. That wasn't reflective of my work ethic overall, and it wasn't true of all the skills my parents had and passed along. I knew how to cook and how to bake, and I had helped take care of Alli and Ben and keep the house clean for years. But why would I bother growing my own vegetables when I could buy them from the cheap market down the street? Why would I spend hours sewing a T-shirt or tank top when I could buy one for $5? Why would I put blood, sweat, and tears into refinishing a piece of furniture when I could buy something new that looked good already? These were the rationalizations I'd made with myself for years. If I could pay for it, I would—and usually with a credit card.

What was worse to think about was the fact that I had spent money to save time and then wasted almost every minute of it. From the age of 14 or 15 on, my life had revolved around television. I knew how many of my favorite shows were on each day and planned my schedule accordingly. Monday, Thursday, and Sunday evenings were filled with at least two or three hour-long programs, so I couldn't do anything then, unless people wanted to come over and watch them together. (Notice Friday and Saturday didn't make that list? It was like television networks knew I had to party on those nights.) Even on other weeknights, I still preferred to be home in time to watch the one show I liked.

My television addiction got worse when seasons of my favorite shows started being released on DVD. I didn't care that I had already seen every episode, I wanted to watch them all again—and I did, often more than once. This was around the same time that the term *binge watch* was popularized, and binge watch I did. I sat on one corner of the brown leather sofa in our basement for so long that it eventually ripped. And the worst part of it all was that the number one excuse I gave my parents for why I couldn't help or learn from them was "I'm too busy." I wasn't too busy to watch *The O.C.* enough times that I could recite almost every word from all four seasons. But I was too busy to let my parents pass down their knowledge to me. I was too busy to spend more quality time with them. I was too busy to create those memories.

I knew I wasn't alone in doing this—"this" being spending hours in front of a television and making the "I'm too busy to do anything else" excuse. Surprisingly, I've learned it's not only a characteristic of my generation, but something that has shifted for many people as electronic devices have become a more prominent part of our lives. At university, one of my favorite classes was on media and cultural studies, and the first aha moment I had in my entire program happened while I was writing a paper for that class on the topic of flow. *Flow*, in media, is another word for programming, and is used to describe the smooth transition networks set up from one television show to another (including the ads in between) to ensure you keep watching what's on that one network. The little splash toward the end of one show that tells you what's coming up next is done for only one reason: to stop you from changing the channel. And it worked on me for years.

One of the best things to come out of being maxed out in 2011 was that it forced me to free up room in my budget, which included canceling my cable. I've never gone back on that decision, and I can't imagine I ever will. Not having cable freed up time that I used to complete my degree, start my blog, change careers, and start freelancing on the side. And even with all of that, I also managed to get outside, go hiking with friends, and spend more time with the people I loved. I was never "too busy." All I had done in the past was choose what I wanted to be busy doing. I had prioritized television over people and, in turn, lost precious time with them. I didn't want to lose another minute, so I decided it was time to finally ask my parents for the help they had once offered.

It started on a day I did know was going to come eventually. I knew that, at some point throughout this year of less, a day would come when something I owned would wear out or fall apart or break, and I would need to replace it. In the end, it turned out the first thing to go was a pair of pajama pants—my only pair of pajama pants. The fabric had caught on something and ripped along one of the seams. My first instinct: throw them out. They were a cheap pair of pajama pants, made of cheap fabric, bought from one of the cheap big-box stores in town. And I was allowed to replace them. So long as I was getting rid of the original item, I could replace anything that needed to be replaced. That was one of the rules. And it wouldn't cost much.

Instead, I acted on a different impulse, which was to ask the women in my family for help—my mom, aunt, grandma, and Alli. "When I come home next month, can you teach me how to sew?" They were surprised but elated. "Of course!" they all responded.

From there, my questions flowed endlessly. *How do you know which thread to use? What happens if you make a mistake? Can I borrow your sewing machine and bring it back to Port Moody with me to play with? Is it possible that I would break it? When is the right time of year to plant cucumber? What about kale, peppers, and tomatoes? Do you think I could set up a container garden on my deck? What size containers would I need? And what kind of soil would I need? Would I also need fertilizer? How much do you think that would cost? When should I pick berries to make jam with? Should I pick them in early August, toward the end of August, or even later than that? How long does it take to make a batch of jam? Will it take a whole weekend or could I do it in a day? And what's the correct ratio of berries to sugar? Now tell me what you know about composting. Do you think I'm allowed to have a small compost container on my deck? What would I do with it when it's full, since my building isn't set up for compost removal?* This went on and on and on. I sounded like a toddler who was trying to understand how the world worked.

Along with asking my parents these questions, I went down the rabbit hole of the Internet and came back up with something I hadn't thought of before. When I first started the shopping ban, I wrote about how I wanted to embrace "minimalism" and learn how to live with less, and I had done that. At this point, I'd taken 54 percent of the belongings out of my home, purchased a few things from the approved shopping list, and stopped myself from making a handful of purchases I didn't need. This felt minimalist enough. I understood the "less" part and I could almost see the light at the end of the tunnel. I knew I could get to the finish line, if I kept doing what I was doing for five more months. But minimalism seemed to be having an identity crisis, because as I looked for tips on how to start small gardens, produce less waste, and be more self-sufficient, I was surprised to also find the term *minimalism* in the articles—only it was being used interchangeably with the term *simple living*. All the articles I read about it reminded me of what my childhood had looked like. I pictured my feet back in the soil, the kitchen table covered in homemade pie crusts, and the cupboard chock-full of canned fruit. I wanted that again. I needed that again.

So I asked more questions and did more research, until I came to the conclusion that, in order to have a simpler life, I would have to change some of the rules for the shopping ban. I wanted to be able to buy supplies for a container garden, so I could plant seeds and grow something myself. I wanted to get all the ingredients that went into making homemade candles, so I could create something beautiful and useful for myself. And I wanted to learn how to make cleaning products, including shampoo and conditioner, so I could prove it was possible and also use fewer chemicals. On the blog, I wrote that I was "upping the ante" in an attempt to challenge myself further, and that wasn't a lie. But the full truth was that I changed the rules in an attempt to get back some of the life I had once known.

**New Rules for the Shopping Ban**

What I'm allowed to shop for:

- Groceries
- Cosmetics and toiletries (only when I run out)
- Gifts for others
- Items on the approved shopping list
- Gardening supplies
- Ingredients for making cleaning products/laundry detergent
- Candle-making supplies

What I'm NOT allowed to shop for:

- Take-out coffee
- Clothes, shoes, accessories
- Books, magazines, notebooks
- Household items (candles, decor, furniture, etc.)
- Electronics
- Basic kitchen supplies (plastic wrap, tin foil, etc.)
- Cleaning products/laundry detergent

# 8

# february: letting go of the future

**months sober:** *25*
**income saved:** *53%*
**total number of belongings tossed:** *60%*

In early February, I went on a solo trip to New York City. It was my third time visiting and would turn out to be my most memorable. As far as travel destinations go, New York City, I have learned, can be done as cheap or as expensive as you want. For this trip, I used travel points to save money on my flight, and stayed on my friend Shannon's couch to save on accommodation. Aside from coffee, food, and one elevator ride up to Top of the

Rock, I didn't spend a penny. And I couldn't, since I wasn't allowed to shop.

What made the trip so memorable was that it overlapped with two other friends' trips to the city. Leanne was a fellow writer in the personal finance space who lived in London, England. What started as two bloggers commenting on each other's posts turned into two friends exchanging lengthy e-mails about money, work, and relationships. David was another Canadian blogger I had connected with only a year before. His writing was fresh and insightful, and gave me so many new ways to think about money, work, and life. The fact that all three of our trips put us in the same place for a few days felt most serendipitous. That is the magic of New York City.

Leanne and I did what tourists do: took pictures of the sun setting over the city from the observation deck at 30 Rock, then sat on the floor in Grand Central Station and took more pictures from the ground up. David and I put serious mileage on our feet, walking from the East Village to the West Village, all along the High Line, through Chelsea, and back to the East Village—with three stops for coffee on our route. It was one of the coldest Februarys on record, but I never minded. I might have not even noticed it, if I hadn't been pulling my hands out of my gloves to check my phone so often.

The whole time I was in New York City, Alli was sending messages with updates about what was happening back at the house. We had learned as kids that when someone in the family was out of town—specifically, when our dad was at sea for work—we shouldn't tell them about any minor arguments or concerns. That person couldn't help to resolve the little things that came up on a daily basis, and hearing about it would only stress them out or cause them to worry. I always thought this was a good lesson for all long-distance relationships. But now it was different. Alli had no one else to talk to. She had no one else to discuss the conversations she had with our mom or dad that left her feeling unsettled. She needed to feel settled. So I never asked her to stop. Instead, I let my fingers go numb every time I pulled my hands out from my gloves to talk to her. And when I returned home, I knew I had to go to Victoria to see things for myself.

My first night at the house was quiet. Our conversations mostly revolved around my trip to New York City and my work. The next day was fine too. Quiet again, but everything else seemed like it was business as usual—typical and routine. My parents sat at the kitchen table together in the morning, while my mom got ready for work and my dad read the news. They drank their coffee and tea, talked, and even laughed. On the third day, I watched them run through this same morning act again and started to wonder what exactly Alli had been so worried about.

That afternoon, I was working in the dining room, frantically scribbling notes on a pad I had taken from the kitchen. When I ran out of space, I flipped the page and found a loose piece of paper that had been slipped into the pad. It was folded in half with the printed text facing me, and the first line read, "How will we divide our assets?"

I stopped breathing. And then a fog poured into the room and blurred my vision and nothing looked the same again.

After reading the entirety of what was on that paper, I knew the truth. Our parents were getting divorced. Then I walked with it out of the dining room, through the kitchen, down the hall, and into Alli's room, where I closed the door and passed it to her with shaky hands.

She screamed and we both burst into tears. Alli had been right. Every ounce of fear and doubt that had been running through her veins had been right. Her gut instinct had been right. I had been wrong. I thought it was impossible since we had just celebrated the best Christmas ever only two months before. I thought it was impossible since our parents had laughed together at the kitchen table that morning. I thought it was impossible since it was us. Our family. The family that talked about everything. Our motto had always been, "There are no secrets in the Flanders family." As it turned out, there was one. The biggest secret was finally out, and now we had to deal with it.

I won't share the details of why my parents split up or how it affected them or my siblings. Those aren't my stories to tell. But I can tell you what it meant for me. After finding the piece of paper and showing it to Alli, we gave it to our parents and had *the* talk. Then we all dispersed and tried to figure out how we individually felt about the news—news we were never supposed to discover through a piece of paper—and all I felt was devastation.

I drove to my friends Travis and Pascal's house to distract myself by playing with their kids, but as soon as they went to bed, I curled up on their couch and started crying. Asking questions aloud, like *What are the next steps? What's going to happen to the house?* It had been in our family since the '50s, and in my own life since 1994. Before my mom met my dad, our life had been anything but stable. She and I lived in seven different homes in the first seven years of my life. I'd changed schools with every new grade I entered—and sometimes changed schools again in the middle of the year, if we moved again. But after Alli was born, we moved into this house and we had been here ever since. Sometimes we swapped bedrooms or moved furniture around, but we never left. I got to stay in one elementary school for the rest of the lower grades, attend one high school, and build friendships that lasted longer than 10 months. We had an open-door policy for family and friends, so there were always people stopping by. And no matter where I moved or traveled, I knew I had a home in this world. We couldn't lose it. I couldn't lose it.

Then I started pleading aloud for a smooth transition and for everyone to be okay. My thoughts jumped ahead and I worried about my parents ending up alone in their own senior years. I didn't want them to separate, but I really, *really* didn't want either of them to be alone. What was going to happen to the dogs? Oh my gosh, the dogs. I hated the thought of our old girls having to enter this uncertain terrain in their senior years. They didn't deal with change well, as it was. How would this affect them?

My cries turned into heavy sobs as I thought of how this could affect my siblings. I had spent my whole life taking care of Alli and Ben—guiding them, and protecting them from confusion and pain every chance I could. I knew we would all handle this situation differently, and I prayed we could stay as neutral as possible and not tear our family apart further by picking sides. But I couldn't guide them this time. They would have to set their own boundaries and make their own rules and manage their own feelings. I couldn't protect them from the effects of this. And they couldn't protect me either—that task was never listed in their job description.

The rest of my tears were for me. I hadn't seen this coming. Even with all of Alli's comments and concerns, I hadn't prepared myself for this. Divorce wasn't supposed to be an option in our family. I was simply not prepared. I also wasn't prepared to deal with it now—in a year that was already full of enough change and challenges, personally and at work. Through all of it, I'd always been able to count on my family being there. Our house. My parents. My half-siblings. My only siblings. The dogs. This was everything that mattered to me, and it all fit under one roof. What if it was never all under the same roof again? How could this be happening?

On the way back to my parents' house, I was driving down the Malahat—a steep portion of Highway 1 that curves in and around the mountain that separates Victoria from the rest of Vancouver Island—when I began to gasp for air. Sweat started to drip down the back of my neck, and I got the sudden urge to pull over and rip my shirt off. But I couldn't. The Malahat only had one lane of traffic going in either direction and no shoulder to pull out on. My heart started racing, and my grip on the steering wheel became slick. *Just breathe, Caitlin. Deep breath in, deep breath out. You're almost there.* I repeated this to myself over and over again for the next four and a half miles. *Deep breath in, deep breath out. You're almost there. You're almost there. You're almost there.* As soon as I could get off the highway, I pulled over, jumped out of my car, and curled up in a ball on the pavement. Feeling the cold move up from the asphalt and into my body helped slow my breath. Then I pulled out my phone and called Clare in Denver. "My parents are getting divorced," I whispered. "And I'm having a panic attack."

It wasn't the first time I'd had a panic attack—or the first time I had called Clare during a panic attack, for that matter. The first two I had were in 2004: one on my second day at a new job, and another on the morning before my third day. I took them both as a sign that it wasn't the right job for me and never went back. The third was in 2013, when I was on a train from downtown St. Louis to Lambert St. Louis Airport. Before the trip, I had been working around the clock, sometimes sitting in front of my computer for 15 hours a day. After taking a few days off to spend time with friends at a blogging conference, I was dreading going back to that schedule. On the train, I felt the familiar and terrifying symptoms creep in. Gasping for air, sweat dripping down the back of my neck, heart racing. *Just breathe, Caitlin. Deep breath in, deep breath out. You're almost there.* When we arrived at the airport, I jumped onto the platform, dropped my bags, and called Clare. I took that one as a sign I needed to work less and establish a healthier routine.

I don't know why I called Clare that first time. We had never even spoken on the phone before, only exchanged e-mails and text messages. But something told me she was the person I needed. Both times I called her, she gave me the same advice: Put your head between your knees and breathe. *Deep breath in, deep breath out.* She repeated this mantra until I caught my breath, at which point I burst into tears and she had to start repeating it again.

This time, when I finally calmed down, I opened my eyes and noticed my surroundings. I was lying on the tiny shoulder of a side street with my car in front of me and a row of newly developed houses on my left. I knew why I'd called Clare this time. Not only was she my debt-free Sober Sally, her parents had also recently gotten divorced. Solidarity, sister. I lay in the dark and stared at the streetlamp standing above me, as Clare asked me questions I didn't have answers to and realized this was just the beginning of the journey. Finding that piece of paper was only the first stop on the map. This panic attack was a sign that I wasn't ready for what was still to come.

Over the next few days, my parents tried to make everything seem like it would be fine. They sat at the kitchen table together in the morning, and we ate dinner together at night. I don't know who was trying harder—us or them—but every interaction felt more like four people trying to dance together around the elephant in the room than a family simply talking. We'd get on the topic of Alli's school, then talk about Ben's school, but *Oh no, Ben isn't here and doesn't know about the divorce yet. We can't talk about Ben. If we talk about Ben, we'll have to talk about the divorce and find out when they are going to tell him. Quick, back away from the elephant.* And then someone would change the subject.

As time went on, these dances started to feel like small wins. My friends would ask how I was doing and I would say, "Well, we've successfully avoided talking about it, so that feels like a win." Eating in the same room together was a win. Talking about what was happening in the news was a win. The real news was happening in our house, but it never came up, and that was the biggest win. These wins felt terrible, of course. There had never been secrets in our family. We talked about and told each other everything. I wanted to ask questions and demand answers and find out if there was a chance this was all a big mistake. Instead, I woke up each morning, got dressed, and joined them in the dance around the elephant. It somehow felt easier to pretend everything would stay the same between us for a little bit longer.

I could only stand to spend a few more days in Victoria before I had to get some space from everything. I felt sick leaving Alli behind to do the dance by herself, and I promised I'd return as often as I could stomach it. For now, I needed to be alone. When I got back to Port Moody, I tried to distract myself by diving into work. Each morning, I got up early, made coffee, and tackled my in-box right away. In my e-mails, I promised to map out new projects and look for more freelance writers and schedule out the blog weeks in advance. But by noon, I was stiff in my chair, staring past my computer screen and into nothing. The fog that filled my parents' house the day I found the piece of paper had followed me home, and I couldn't see anything in front of me. By 2 P.M., I had usually carried my laptop to the couch, convincing myself I'd get more done if I were comfortable. At 4 P.M., I logged off, grateful if I'd accomplished anything at all. And then I ate dinner and crawled into bed.

My bed was supposed to be my sanctuary. After Chris and I had broken up so many years before, I had bought everything I would need for my bed to be my sanctum—a sacred place to seek refuge from the day. And in the fall, I had finally replaced my 13-year-old mattress, using money from the shopping ban account.

Emma and I described new beds with clean bedding as marshmallows, and getting into them meant we had achieved marshmallow status. I started sending those two words to her in a text message shortly after dinner each day. By 7 P.M., the dishes were done and I had achieved marshmallow status. Sometimes I would stare at the books on my nightstand and consider reading them while cocooned in my marshmallow, but it always felt like too much work. Picking one up and having to hold it in front of me felt like too much work. So I left them alone to do nothing, and curled up to do nothing myself.

At first, Emma would tell me she was jealous of how much time I was spending in bed. I announced it like it was a point of pride—my greatest achievement each day. "I'm done with everything! It's marshmallow time." But even with the ferry boat ride and 75 miles of distance between us, she knew I was seeking refuge before I did. I started crawling in a little earlier each day. My office and the living room felt too open. I didn't want to be out in the open. I wanted to hide—from my life, from my family, from the truth. I didn't want it to be real, so I went to bed, where I could curl up and pretend like everything was okay. Soon 7 o'clock became 6 o'clock, and 6 o'clock became 5. Emma was concerned with my behavior. Eventually I brought dinner to bed, and only left the room to do the dishes. It didn't take long before I stopped doing even that, and let the dishes pile up atop the stack of books on my nightstand instead. The day I ran out of space to set my coffee mug so I could work from bed was the first day I got mad.

On impulse, I stormed back and forth between the bedroom and kitchen, carrying dishes out and throwing them into the sink. I stripped the bed naked and filled the washing machine with linens and detergent. I sprayed down the bathroom and wiped every surface in the apartment clean. My life was enough of a mess. I did not need to make it worse by living in one too.

When I was done, I walked back into my bedroom and looked at the stack of books. They were the same books I had placed there months before, occasionally shuffling the order in which I might read them, but never actually reading them. Every time I looked at them, I felt sorry for the words and the authors, and ashamed for not reading enough. I loved to read. I had grown up with books practically sewn to my hands. On trips, I always brought at least three with me. But I never read anymore. My nightstand had become an invisible corner in my home—a place where you grow accustomed to the mess, even though you feel guilty every time you look at it. I couldn't handle any more feelings of guilt, so I brought them back to the bookshelf where they belonged.

Each book had a home inside my home. My shelves were still organized by genre—fiction, memoirs, business, and personal finance—and then by size. There were visible spaces for me to slip each one back in, to make the collection look complete. But as I looked at each one, I realized it had been more than six months since my first declutter and purge, and I still owned dozens of books I hadn't read. In fact, there were lots of things in my apartment I had kept but still hadn't used. I could've broken it down by room for a blog post, and listed off what was in my bedroom, kitchen, living room, office, and bathroom for readers. But there were really only two categories I could see: the stuff I used, and the stuff I wanted the ideal version of myself to use.

The stuff I wanted the ideal version of myself to use was everything I had once bought in hopes that it would somehow make my life or myself better. There were books I thought smart Cait should read, clothes I thought professional Cait would wear, projects I thought creative Cait could tackle. Classic novels, little black dresses, scrapbook materials, and more. At one point, I'd put thousands of dollars on my credit cards for this stuff—stuff I purchased with every intention of using, but only because I told myself it would somehow help. I wasn't good enough, but this stuff would make me better. I wanted to read, wear, and do everything so I could become the person I thought I should be. Having these items in my home proved it was possible. I would do it all one day, and become a better person one day. This time, one day never came.

Up until this point, the only two questions I'd been asking myself when I decluttered my belongings were *Have I used this recently?* and *Do I plan to use this soon?* If the answers were yes, I kept it. If I thought it had a purpose in my life, I kept it. My friends would ask how I'd been able to get rid of so much stuff, and the question always confused me. I literally didn't use 56 percent of what I had once owned. Why would it be hard to get rid of it? But the stuff that remained for the ideal version of myself was different. I could now see what it was, and once you see the truth you can't unsee it. I had to accept the fact that I was never going to be the type of person who read, wore, and did these things. But that still doesn't mean it was easy to let go of.

I started with the books and asked myself a question I'd never considered the answer to before: *Who are you buying this for: the person you are, or the person you want to be?* This should've been the question I'd asked before buying each and every one of them. This should've been the question I'd asked before buying anything. The answer, in many cases, was that I had bought it for the person I was, but there were at least a dozen books I had bought because I thought they were the types of books a smarter version of myself would read. I moved into the bedroom and asked the same question of my clothes. And after walking through every room, I had filled a few small bags with things to let go of. I had to let go of the stuff I wanted the ideal version of myself to use, and accept myself for who I really was.

And when I was done, I had to let go of something that was even bigger than myself: my family.

It came in waves. I would mask the pain with my warm comforter, then remember something else I had to let go of. Like the family trip to Hawaii we had planned to go on when Ben was done with his undergraduate degree in 2019. We had only been on two trips together as a family: one to Disneyland in 2004 and one to Mexico in 2011. Now those two trips would be the only two trips we would ever go on. Then I would think ahead to situations I had always assumed would be possible. Like having a house where Alli, Ben, and I could bring our future kids, where we could all be under one roof. What was it going to be like for our kids to have different sets of grandparents? Would we need to have separate birthdays, holidays, and Christmases? What would it be like at our weddings, if any of us got married? Would our parents even be on speaking terms?

I had always assumed it would be more difficult for a young child to have parents separate, but I learned your age only changes the ways in which you are impacted. If you're young enough to not remember your parents ever being together, it's all you'll ever know. But when you're an adult (and practically a co-parent), and you grew up in a loving household, your parents' divorce can feel like your own divorce. And there is a lot to let go of when you find out it's over.

Even after cleaning the apartment and decluttering more of my belongings, I made my bed and crawled back in. There, I grieved the loss of the family I'd known—the traditions, the rituals, and the secret language only the five of us knew. This wasn't like any other pain I'd experienced. There were no pangs or stings. My bones didn't ache. It didn't feel like a usual breakup. It didn't even compare to a death in the family. It was a death of the whole unit, and the future I thought we were going to have.

I had always assumed my parents would be together forever. Nothing had ever made me think otherwise. And nothing had ever prepared me for how to deal with all the loss that would come with a divorce. There was a tectonic shift in the rock we all stood on and now we were on unstable ground. I had to let go of everything I had once thought was true and accept our new reality. It wasn't easy, and I knew this was only the beginning of the journey. So I stayed in bed a little longer, cried a lot harder, and repeated the mantra over and over to myself when I needed to.

*Deep breath in, deep breath out.*
*Deep breath in, deep breath out.*

# 9

# march: lightening up

**months sober:** *26*
**income saved:** *34%*
**confidence I can complete this project:** *70%*

I wish I could say that's where I left my pain: back in February, where it had first started. I wish I could say I discovered the one secret that was being kept in our family, had a panic attack and cried a little, then let go and gotten over it. It would have felt so good to package it up as the worst month of my life, wrap a black bow around it, and ship it off for good. Of course, it's never quite that simple. We like to believe each month of the year is one chapter of our lives, but this one carried over and the divorce consumed mine. The frequency with which I would break down and sob midsentence slowed, but only because I was paralyzed with pain. I had skipped the bargaining stage of grief. There was nothing to bargain for. I knew my parents weren't going back on their decision, and there was nothing I could do to change that. Instead, I slipped right from anger into depression.

I don't use the word *depression* lightly; I would never use that word lightly. Yes, it's the label for one of the five stages of grief, but I know how serious depression is. Growing up, I witnessed a family friend struggle with clinical depression that crippled her for years. There was also bipolar and manic depression in our family. I would never compare the sadness you can slip into after suffering a loss to those forms of depression. It's not the same, not even close. But it was perhaps because I knew how serious depression was that it took me nearly two months to tell someone how deep and penetrating my pain had been.

I could barely get out of bed—and not because bed was my sanctuary. There was nothing beautiful or peaceful about living under the covers in pajamas that hadn't been washed in weeks. There was simply no better place to spend half the day in the fetal position. When friends would send text messages or try to call and check in on me, I ignored them. *Why had I told so many people about this?* I would ask myself. *I don't want to talk about it anymore. Please stop asking how I'm doing,* I prayed every time my phone lit up. *I am terrible and I don't want to talk about it anymore.*

Emma and Clare were the only two people I let in. Emma, because I knew I could say anything and she wouldn't judge me. Clare, because I knew she had fought the same fight before. Most of the addicts I've met are sensitive to pain, which is why we try to hide from it. So long as I was honest with Emma and Clare, I wasn't hiding from the pain—I just didn't want the whole world to know how much it hurt.

The longer I ignored everyone else, the more comforting messages they sent through. There were the usual "It's going to get better!" condolences. A few people sent religious and spiritual messages—verses from the Bible about sympathy and strength, and wise words on letting go and finding happiness from Buddhism. One friend suggested I try meditating, so I downloaded the Calm app on my phone so it could guide me. I only tried it once and was so uncomfortable being alone with my thoughts that I turned it off three minutes in. It would be another two years before I tried again and finally started my meditation practice. In the meantime, the best thing to come from that app was discovering I could use it to listen to the sound of rain. Growing up in the Pacific Northwest, I had always found rain soothing. I think you have to in order to survive here. With the phone on my nightstand, I left the app open and relaxed into the first night of good sleep I'd had in weeks. Maybe rain was my religion.

The most troubling thought that ran through my mind during this time wasn't about the divorce itself. It wasn't about my parents or our family or the future. It was about drinking. I didn't shop or even think about shopping. But I did think about drinking. There were many nights when I had to talk myself out of going downstairs to the liquor store in my building and bringing home a bottle of wine. *I live alone. No one will ever know.* There it was again: the voice—my voice—trying to talk me into doing something bad. The rationalizing got more intense, as I reminded myself none of my friends lived close by, and I'd been ignoring everyone lately anyway. *Seriously, no one would know.* If I'd only been sober for a few months, I would've been at a much higher risk of giving in to these thoughts. But I knew I'd worked through pain without alcohol before, and I was determined to do it again. This was the first time I ever considered going to an AA meeting.

I can't really say anything about Alcoholics Anonymous, because I have no experience with it. My only knowledge of what took place in meetings came from stories told by my dad and one other friend who got sober six months before me. My dad only went to meetings for the first year of his sobriety, then felt that continuing to go served no purpose. His thought: Why stay in the continuous loop of talking about living with addiction when you could simply go out and live? My friend, on the other hand, was more than three years sober and still went on a weekly basis. I don't think either of their decisions was right or wrong, so long as it was right for them.

AA had never felt like it was right for me. I probably could have stood to go at least once. Considering how many times I'd been labeled as "the sober one" and felt left out of the group, I probably could have used a few more sober friends in my life. In fact, I'm certain I needed more sober friends in my life. But something about AA never felt right. Maybe it was the religious aspect. I didn't subscribe to any doctrine and, therefore, I wasn't comfortable with all the guiding principles, or 12 steps. I thought the order in which they were listed was perfect, but they were written in a language that was foreign to me. I remembered reading the Serenity Prayer once and finding I could only relate to two lines: "Living one day at a time / Enjoying one moment at a time." I also wasn't comfortable with the gender bias in most of the language. I'm sure I could have found modern AA meetings that would have been happy to swap things out or rewrite the whole list, but I didn't want to demand that. Who was I to say a practice that had been helping people since 1935 should be altered for me?

I shared my struggles with Clare and asked if she had ever been to a meeting before. She had gone to one, and her experience matched everything I felt, which was that it wasn't right for me. She still encouraged me to go, but I stubbornly refused and committed to work through the thoughts on my own. I didn't have faith in much, but the little bit I did have left was sitting on my shoulder, encouraging me to live one day at a time and enjoy one moment at a time.

There was a big difference between thinking about drinking now compared to when I thought about it after I first quit. It was no longer a habit or routine for me. I wasn't stuck in the cycle of craving it, drinking it, and feeling ashamed about it. I wasn't jonesing for a blackout, and my eyes weren't twitching at the thought of having to struggle through this without booze. I knew I didn't actually want to drink or deal with any of the consequences that would come from ending my sobriety. I was just tired of being in pain. Pain—both emotional and physical—was exhausting. I couldn't get out of bed because dealing with the pain took all of my energy, and I had nothing left in me. Once upon a time, drinking had felt like the eraser for all pain, the same way spending money had felt like the path to a bigger and better life. I wasn't in the habit of doing either now, and I was better for it.

But that doesn't mean I didn't give in to other cravings.

While many people treat themselves by buying things, I had always treated myself with food. So instead of picking up a bottle of wine, I picked up pizza. And chocolate. And ice cream. And some nights, I picked up pizza, chocolate, and ice cream. There was nothing mindless about it—I knew I was eating my feelings. I would place the order and walk into the stores knowing I was buying things that would allow me to eat my feelings. I didn't do it every night, and I didn't eat it all in one sitting. These weren't the same binges I'd done before. I didn't want to overdose on cheese or go into a sugar coma. I simply wanted a little comfort, every few days, and finding it in food seemed like the healthiest option.

On those same nights, I usually chased the food with a binge of Netflix. The stack of books on my nightstand had felt too heavy to pick up, but turning on Netflix was easy—too easy. I was exhausted from the pain, and sick of hearing the thoughts that raced through my mind. So as soon as I came home with the food, I started wherever I had left off during my last binge and let the show play until I went to bed.

There is something to be said about being totally self-aware and still choosing to do what you know is bad for you. On the one hand, I could argue that I was perhaps weak or still had yet to be cured of feeling like I could get through tough situations without the help of a substance. But on the other hand, this was the first time I had been aware of what I was doing while I was doing it. Before this, I had never swallowed a pizza or drunk a bottle of wine while thinking, "I'm in a lot of pain right now, and this is going to temporarily relieve me from it." I just ate and got blackout drunk. It wasn't until I was sober and had to feel my way through every minute of discomfort that I realized why I had been shoving these things down my throat for all those years.

This was different. I wasn't shoving food down or swallowing anything whole. And I wasn't hiding it this time. In fact, I sent pictures of all my unhealthy eating choices to Emma, whenever I decided to make them. I told her I refused to feel guilty, and I meant it. I didn't feel guilty and I didn't shame myself after. I never wanted to fall back into a cycle of self-loathing. Instead, it was almost like I was testing another theory. The religious passages and wise words and meditation weren't helping. I wasn't going to drink and there was nothing I wanted to buy. But if 80 percent of my eating decisions were good, wasn't that good enough? Couldn't I treat myself just a little bit?

Admittedly, this wasn't the best idea I'd ever had. However, there was still a reason I told Emma, over anyone else—because she firmly fell into the camp of friends who encourage people to make good choices. I knew she would let me off the hook for a little while, but she would also be there when I was ready to get back on track. She let me be sad and listened to me vent for months, but she only let me eat pizza, chocolate, and ice cream for a couple of weeks before saying something. "You'll feel better if you eat better, hon." And I knew she was right. Not just because it was bad for me, but because I'd been paying attention to how my body was reacting after eating it all.

Every time I ate too much white sugar or white flour, I crashed—hard. I would feel chilled, start shivering, and curl up with a blanket. Then I would wake up and wonder how I had just lost an hour of my day and why I felt hung over. These weren't naps. I wasn't catching up on sleep or listening to my body and getting rest. My body was doing the talking, and it was telling me it couldn't handle what I was putting into it. There was type 2 diabetes in my family, so I knew the warning signs. If I wasn't careful, I could develop it—and that was not a disease I wanted to spend the rest of my life managing.

In noticing this pattern, I started taking notes about how I felt after eating certain foods and slowly decreased my intake of all the ones that made me feel sick. It wasn't a diet. I spent a year tracking what I was eating and counting calories, which was also a key part of the way I'd lost 30 pounds in 2012. That had been a diet, and I wouldn't do it again, or any other diet for that matter. This was not a diet. I didn't want to lose weight or change anything about my body. I simply wanted to feel better. It seemed the healthiest thing I could do was be aware of how foods made me feel, and eat less of what made me feel sick and more of what gave me good energy.

The process of tracking what I was eating and eliminating what didn't make me feel good was identical to what I had done when I decided to get out of debt. I tracked my spending every day, finally saw where my money was going, and only then was I able to ask myself how I felt about the numbers. Was I comfortable spending all of that money? Did the things I spent money on add value to my life? If the answer was yes, I kept it in the budget. But if I felt like I wanted to put more toward debt repayment, I cut back and moved things around to make it happen. The process I used to set up the shopping ban, and later change the rules, was similar. I decided I could keep spending money on things that added value to my life, like travel, but I would cut back on everything else so I could learn how to live with less and save more. Then I took inventory of my belongings, committed to only buying a few necessities, and saved a lot of money—and potential waste—as a result.

All of these discoveries could have been boiled down to two questions: If it didn't feel good, why would I do it?

And what did I really want right now? To feel good—or at least, to feel better.

While the comfort food phase took only a couple of weeks to reverse, my newly rediscovered television addiction required a little more turnaround time—31 days, to be exact. What started as background noise that filled the silent void in my evenings had quickly become nonstop chatter. I had always loved living alone, but I did not love *being* alone now, and there was a big difference. Living alone meant I had the freedom to do whatever I wanted in my own space, without having to think about how it would affect someone else. Being alone meant not having someone else to share my daily life with. As someone who gets a lot of energy from conversations and connections, having a roommate or partner in the same space might have dramatically changed what this period of my life looked like. Since I didn't have that, though, I turned on Netflix and let the voices from some of my favorite shows keep me company.

It started with the evenings. When I'd begun working remotely, two years before, I had promised myself I wouldn't let my days be filled with distractions, including television. I kept that promise, and only occasionally watched TV at night. When the fog entered my life and followed me home, however, I started turning on my television at the same time I closed my work laptop. A minute of silence felt too painful to live through, so I kept the noise going until bedtime. Eventually, I couldn't handle the silence at bedtime either, so I let shows stream on the laptop in my bedroom all night. Sometimes, I woke up at 2 or 3 in the morning and groggily shut it down. More often than not, though, Netflix was the first tab I saw open on my laptop in the morning, so I would hit play and let the voices keep me company as I made coffee and got ready for the day.

There was nothing intentional about this. It was completely mindless—a way to avoid the discomfort I didn't want to face. I wasn't even paying attention to the shows I was watching. I wasn't watching them. The characters' voices were just keeping me company. Still, I managed to get through seven seasons of one show and nine seasons of another. More than 250 hours of television—10.4 days, or 2.9 percent of my year. I knew things had to change when I started leaving it on at all hours. I was having trouble focusing during the day, losing motivation to work on my blog and freelance in the evening, and having trouble sleeping at night. The silence would hurt, but the noise had to go.

I decided to do what I often did in these situations: challenge myself to go without something for a set length of time—in this case, one month, or 31 days. Not surprisingly, I experienced many of the same physical reactions to the television ban as I had with the shopping and take-out coffee ban. On day one, I felt the usual pang to watch television when I sat down to eat dinner and crawled into bed at night. Days two and three were the same. These were habits I had built into my daily life that now needed to be replaced with something else. I changed the rules so I was allowed to watch TED Talks in these instances. I also started listening to more podcasts and audiobooks, which was something I'd been telling myself I "didn't have time to do" for far too long. I did have the time, I had just chosen to spend it doing other things. I still don't understand why we are always so quick to push off the things we actually enjoy doing for the things that take just a little less effort. It wasn't until I started asking myself what I wanted right now—to feel better—that I stopped making excuses and allocated more time to reading.

Throughout the month, I read five books and listened to countless episodes of various podcasts. I also wrote half a dozen blog posts, and had as many meetings with a friend who was going to help me bring some ideas for the blog to life. To go along with the new rules for the shopping ban, I started researching the zero-waste movement and coming up with ideas for how I could slowly start to reduce mine. I spent time outdoors, going for walks alone and hikes with friends. I had two mentoring sessions with women I looked up to, and caught up with even more friends on the phone or video chat. And after hearing about it from my friend David, whom I'd spent time with in New York City, I tested my ability to handle 90 minutes of peace and quiet by going "floating" in a sensory deprivation tank. It felt good. I had gotten out of bed and lived my life, and it felt good.

That's not to say the ban felt like a complete success. I watched probably a dozen hours of television that month, and changed the rules again so I could watch two documentaries. It also didn't cure all of my troubles with focusing and sleeping. But I wasn't mindlessly consuming television for the sake of avoiding the uncomfortable silence anymore. It was intentional. I knew exactly what I wanted to watch, and I set aside the time to watch it. Before the month was even over, I knew this was how I wanted to continue in the future. I also knew I had to reset my boundaries, so I would watch only after work and before bed. I could live with the silence. What I couldn't live with was losing hours, days, and weeks of my life to things that didn't matter.

As I became more mindful about what I was putting into my body and mind, I started noticing I had become a lot more mindful about my spending, specifically when it came to things I was allowed to purchase. When I first wrote the approved shopping list, I had wondered if it would make things too easy. If having a list of things I was allowed to buy during the year in which I was not allowed to buy things was a cop-out. I also worried that being allowed to purchase some things would lure me into purchasing more things that weren't on the list. I never imagined the exact opposite might be true, and that the list would actually force me to make smarter spending decisions overall.

Because I was only allowed to buy one new sweatshirt, as an example, it had to be the best. Not the best brand or the most expensive or the highest quality. It had to be the best for me. It had to fit right and feel good and be something I could imagine wearing almost every day, because that's what all the items in my new, tiny wardrobe did—they were worn almost every day. I tried on sweatshirts that looked like my style but fit all wrong. I tried on more that looked like they would fit but then were too tight in my hips and too big in my chest (a common problem when you're curvy yet also have basically no breasts). I tried on green sweatshirts and blue sweatshirts and black sweatshirts and gray sweatshirts. All my usual standard colors, but nothing was good enough. In the end, a maroon-colored zip-up finally crossed off all the boxes. It was the first one I could see myself wearing often, the first one I could imagine spending money on, and it took me nine months to find it. There was nothing impulsive about that decision.

I went through the same process when I was picking out the one outfit I would wear to multiple weddings, the one pair of pants I would wear at the gym, and the one pair of boots I would use in the cooler weather. Knowing I could purchase only one of each of those things made the decisions so much more difficult—and so much more meaningful. I thought back to the four black garbage bags full of clothes I had gotten rid of only months before, and remembered how uncomfortable I felt wearing most of those items. I didn't want to waste my money on anything that didn't cover up enough, or hugged the wrong curves, or didn't feel like me. I wanted to feel good—in the clothes I was wearing, and in my decisions to spend money on them.

It turned out the approved shopping list was almost like my insurance policy on the whole experiment. It covered a few purchases, and gave me permission to replace things as I needed them—and there were two things I finally ended up having to replace in the spring. The cell phone that constantly turned itself off did so for the last time and never came back on again. I couldn't live without a phone, so I had to go shopping. I didn't buy the newest or most expensive model. My decision to shop wasn't the result of a product release or an advertisement or a sales promotion. I bought what I needed and what I could afford. And then the one and only pair of jeans I owned ripped in the inner thigh. I put my new sewing skills to work and attempted to fix it, but learned after only seven days that there is no permanent way to fix holes in denim that gets stretched around your thigh—at least not that will look good. After ripping through the two patch jobs I had done, I went back out and bought one new pair of jeans.

It dawned on me that I had never shopped like this before. I had never truly felt a need for something, because I had always purchased things to fill future needs that might come up. Like using coupons to buy two bottles of shower gel, even though I already had some at home, because I would still need more one day. Or buying a shirt I liked in four colors, in case I couldn't find one that fit right ever again. I convinced myself these things would never be on sale again, so I should buy them while they were cheap. Advertisements and marketing campaigns had conditioned me to believe everything was now or never. It never occurred to me to wait until I actually needed something. The truth, I was learning, was that we couldn't actually discover what we needed until we lived without it.

# 10

# april: planning my exit

**months sober:** *27*
**income saved:** *38%*
**total number of belongings tossed:** *65%*

Amid everything else that was going on, my gut was telling me to be prepared for more change. It was the same gut instinct that told me I was getting close to being maxed out in 2011, and the same gut instinct that told me I needed to stop drinking months before I took my last sip. This time, it was telling me to stockpile my cash and build up my emergency fund. The future was uncertain and I would need it.

I didn't know what to make of this, at first. Since paying off my debt in 2013, I'd always had some cash on hand. There was a $500-to-$1,000 buffer in my checking account at all times, and another $2,000 to $3,000 in savings. Everything else was being funneled directly into my retirement accounts. I had felt good about this strategy and comfortable with my financial situation, overall. But I wouldn't argue with my gut. I did know the future was uncertain, right now. I didn't know why I would need extra money, but I wouldn't argue with my gut.

I had at least a dozen conversations with friends about this, asking if they'd ever felt the same and what it had meant for them. The few who'd experienced it all agreed the feeling of needing to stockpile cash had occurred in a time of crisis. Their own divorces, deaths in the family, job layoffs. Situations that ripped the path they had been walking on up from the ground and forced them to carve out a new one. Of course, my parents' divorce had ripped up the path my family had been walking on, but it wasn't going to affect my finances. Everything else felt uncertain, but I knew this much was true.

The only other crisis I could see myself entering was at work. Since the Christmas party, I had felt more disconnected from the company I worked for than ever. I knew my role and I did my job. But with the company's sudden growth, our job descriptions had been solidified and I was pigeonholed into doing things I didn't like—things that didn't align with my morals and values anymore. I spoke up in meetings, but if my ideas didn't match with marketing and search engine optimization (SEO) campaigns, I was quickly shot down. My opinion didn't matter anymore—but it should have. Everyone's opinion should have. That was one of the things I had loved most when the core six worked together in the townhouse. We all swapped hats and our work mattered.

It didn't help that I was suffering from occupational burnout. Working remotely for two years might have looked like a dream on the outside, but it came with some difficult and often unspoken truths. The first was that it had taken almost those entire two years to create any kind of healthy routine. After having the panic attack in St. Louis in 2013, I knew I had to start working less and taking better care of myself, but it was a constant work in progress. I was doing a good job of starting at a regular hour, and taking coffee and lunch breaks, but I was still working too much.

Another common problem that not enough people discuss is how being given the opportunity to work remotely comes with a certain kind of guilt. Since no one can physically see you in person, you feel the need to be online and available at all times, to prove you are, in fact, working. Having the added responsibility of being in a management position only made this worse, and meant I was often online and available for 10 to 12 hours each day.

If I'm honest, this is one of the biggest issues friends and I have faced when working for startups, in general. Whether you work remotely or in the office, there is an understanding that you should be as committed to the company as the CEO—that means working long hours, and giving up parts of your life, in order to see the company succeed. Some companies compensate their employees generously for this level of commitment, but many do not. In fact, I know a handful of companies that take advantage of the people who want all the other "benefits" that come with working for startups—the food and alcohol, game rooms, yoga studios, gym passes, and free transit—and pay them lower, sometimes unlivable wages. People accept this, and trade their time and energy for it, because they think it's worth it to say they've worked for a specific company or gotten a certain type of experience.

The startup I worked for compensated me fairly, but that didn't change the fact I was still suffering from burnout. I never wanted to admit it, but I was exhausted. I was discouraged by the work I was doing, disappointed by the communication with team members, and frustrated with the lack of interest when I expressed any of these concerns. And I was tired of exchanging 50 to 60 hours of every week for it all.

I didn't realize how unhappy I was until one sunny afternoon in April, when I found myself giving my computer screen the middle finger while cursing out loud and crying. This was something I had been doing for weeks: giving my computer screen the middle finger while cursing out loud, that is. The crying was new. The divorce had turned me into a regular sobber, and that could have been partially to blame. But I also knew I'd hit my breaking point, and staying was doing more harm than good. My happiness finally outweighed my loyalty to my boss and my desire for steady paychecks. I needed to quit my job.

Up until that point, I hadn't given much thought to what I would do next in my career. Three years before, I had never imagined my path would have taken me to this place to begin with. I had always loved writing, but graduated from high school thinking I should do something more practical—something stable where I could earn a decent income. *I'll become an accountant,* I thought. I'd aced my two accounting courses in high school, so that would be the profession for me. One semester of the business program at our local college proved that would, in fact, not be the profession for me. The only class I actually enjoyed was marketing, so I dropped out of the business program and pursued my degree in communications instead.

While studying communications, I landed an internship with the provincial government. For three months, I worked as a junior communications officer. My job involved writing media alerts, press releases, and speeches for cabinet ministers. There were things I loved about the position—namely that I got to spend my days researching and writing. Someone was actually paying me to write! And there was something to be said about knowing that someone in a position of power was reading the words you wrote for them. But being paid to write was not enough to make me forget the list of things I disliked about the job, which included the long hours (starting at 6 A.M.), late evenings (leaving at 6 P.M.), and subject matter (boring). Still, when I graduated, I assumed this was the position I would try to get permanently and the career ladder I would climb. I would be a junior communications officer in my 20s, communications officer in my 30s, communications manager in my 40s, and communications director before I retired. For someone who'd grown up in Victoria, which is a government town, getting in early would be like winning the career jackpot. I would work for 35 years and retire with a pension, just like my parents had. That was the plan.

Of course, things don't always go to plan, which I have learned can sometimes be a good thing. If things had gone to plan, I might not have spent the first five years of my career working in education publishing. I might not have worked with some of the most talented teachers I've ever met, and learned the ins and outs of instructional design. And then I might not have found the rungs pulled out of my career ladder during a two-year hiring freeze within the government, which caused me to feel stuck and finally consider leaving the public sector. If things had gone to plan, I might not have started my blog. I might not have connected with a reader who would eventually offer me a full-time job as the managing editor of her website. And I might never have had the opportunity to learn from her, and have her encourage me to continue pursuing every opportunity my blog had provided me.

My boss took a huge chance on hiring me—the "blonde on a budget" she had never met in person. I was grateful for everything she had done for me, but also felt indebted to her for believing in me. This is why I stuck it out for so long—because my boss had believed in me, and I felt like I owed her. Like she had spent good money on me, at one point, and I had to fulfill my purpose.

I had never made a plan for what I would do next, because I had never thought about leaving before. I was happy—until I wasn't. I thought I would stay and help the company continue to grow—until I couldn't. If I wanted to do something more, I would have to do it elsewhere, but I didn't know where elsewhere was or what I wanted to do. It wasn't until my friend Kayla, in Denver, told me how unhappy she was at her job and that she'd promised herself she would quit by July 1 that I realized I needed to do the same. I needed an end date. I needed to be able to see a light at the end of this tunnel and know I'd come out on the other side.

July 1 felt too soon. There were projects I really did want to see through to their ends, and a trip to Toronto already booked for May. My gut also told me July 1 was too soon because I needed more time to save money and come up with a plan. I didn't know what I was going to do next, but I knew I couldn't stay in this job all year. No amount of money was worth the tears I was shedding each week. If that meant I had to quit without a new job, I would do it.

After running some numbers, I settled on September 1. Five months would be enough time to find a new job, and also to boost my savings so I had at least six months of living expenses in the bank if I needed it. I would quit in August and be done working for the company by September 1. That was the plan.

However, I decided to also set a stretch goal for myself. Stretch goals were something I had first learned about through reading personal finance blogs. People set them to challenge themselves to accomplish something even faster than they thought they could—by stretching their limits, so to speak. I had set stretch goals to pay off my debt sooner. The original plan had been to pay it off in three years, then two and a half, and I ended up doing it in two. I had also set stretch goals when I was losing weight and again when I was training for my first half marathon. Now I would set another stretch goal, in hopes it would motivate me to do whatever it took to get myself out of this situation. July 1 felt too soon, but I wrote it on a piece of paper and taped it to my computer so I could look at it each day. September 1 would be a fine end date, but July 1 would be even better.

The other truth that revealed itself to me, while making this decision, was that I didn't need as much money as I used to. Before the shopping ban, the most I was saving was 10 percent of my income each month, which meant I'd been spending the other 90 percent. One of my goals for the ban was to learn how to live on less money, so I could save more—and I had been doing that. Most months, I was saving between 20 and 30 percent of my income. In January and February, I saved 56 percent and 53 percent respectively, which meant I only needed 44 to 47 percent of my income to cover my living expenses. I had proven my theory: I could, in fact, live on far less money than I used to—and save and travel.

I wish I could say this didn't feel as revelatory as it did. With these new numbers in hand, I literally fantasized about screaming my discovery from the rooftops of stores and shopping malls. *If you're wondering why you can't save money, stop buying stuff you don't need! And trust me, you probably don't need anything in here!* This should have been obvious. I had been writing about money for almost four years at this point, and paid down nearly $30,000 of debt and started saving for retirement in that time. I should have known I didn't need a lot of money to achieve my financial goals. However, I had also always been stuck in the consumerism cycle. I thought I needed to earn more money each year, so I could have more of what I wanted. That cycle meant I was constantly spending the extra money I was earning, rather than saving it, and I still wanted more on top of that. But the ban proved another theory: When you want less, you consume less—and you also need less money.

I asked Kayla what she was going to do after she quit her job, and she said she was going back to being a full-time freelance writer. She had done it before and had a few struggles, but felt she'd learned a lot in the years that had passed and wanted to try it again. Aside from being proud of her, I was jealous of her courage. Quitting to go out on her own felt fearless and heroic. She knew exactly what she wanted and she was going for it.

When Kayla asked what I wanted to do next, I admitted I didn't know. I had started looking at job boards and nothing felt right yet. The salaries were fine but the companies didn't interest me and the job descriptions sounded less than thrilling. She stopped me midsentence. "But what do you really *want* to do?"

This was a question I had never asked myself. Every position I'd ever taken was for either the experience or the salary, and I was never happy in any of them. I would say things like, "It's okay for now," while I counted down the hours until I could clock out for the day. And I had always felt strapped to my desk, because I needed a steady paycheck for all my bills and debt repayment. I would buy things because I thought they would help me become a better version of myself, and I would take jobs with higher salaries because I needed to pay for it all. I had never stopped to ask myself what I really wanted, probably because I'd never been in a position where I could afford to.

One of the best things about budgeting and keeping a record of where your money goes is that it gives you the tools to map out a plan for the big stuff—like quitting your job. I could look ahead and calculate that it would take me five months to save up enough that I would feel comfortable quitting. But when I looked back at all my budgets from the first nine months of the ban, one other number stood out from all of them: I was spending almost the exact same amount of money on living expenses every month—and it was less than ever before. The reason my percentages fluctuated was because of all the travel I had been doing, which was a luxury and could be cut from my budget if I didn't have the money for it. Everything else fit into one newer, much smaller number—and that number also happened to be the exact same amount of money I was already earning through freelance writing every month.

When Kayla first told me she was going to be a full-time freelance writer, it hadn't dawned on me that I might actually be able to do the same thing one day. Working for myself had never been part of the plan. I knew a long list of bloggers who'd launched their websites in hopes they would one day make enough money to quit their jobs and do it full time. That had never been part of my plan. I started my blog to document my debt-repayment journey. It was an accountability tool, and a way to connect with people who were dealing with similar situations. Along the way, I had made a few connections and picked up some freelance work, but it was always something I did on the side. Working for myself had never been part of the plan before—but it was an option now.

The shopping ban showed me I was already earning the exact amount of money freelancing that I needed to cover my living expenses. It also showed me the full amount I would need to earn if I wanted to save (including setting money aside for taxes) and still travel. I wasn't exactly comfortable with the idea of taking a pay cut, but the ban proved I could afford to. If you want more stuff, you need to earn more money. If you want less, you need less—and are then able to calculate how much money you actually need to earn. I could afford to earn less than my current salary, and I was willing to risk that if it meant I could create a job I actually wanted.

So that became the new plan: I would find a couple more clients, and then quit my job to focus on my blog and my freelance writing. It was a calculated risk, but I knew it was one worth taking.

From that day on, I started reading the latest books and blog posts about working for yourself, and listening to a couple of podcasts on the same topic. Continuing with what I had learned during the TV ban, I was consuming media (including podcasts) only after work and before 9 P.M., so it wouldn't disrupt my routine or my sleep—and I tried not to binge. However, unlike the weeks and months of my life I had wasted watching seasons of shows and reality television, I was actually getting something out of this content, and I needed every piece of the advice.

While listening to one podcast, in particular, I would find myself taking mental notes about things I should do to grow my business. Then I would hit pause, search for any piece of paper I could find, and scribble everything down. Within a few weeks, my apartment was littered with scraps of paper, library books, and return-date notices. I had also ripped blank pieces of paper out of an old drawing book, taped them to the wall, and created a messy timeline of what I wanted to accomplish before I quit. My apartment didn't look as tidy as it had in the pictures I'd shared on my blog in October, but I didn't mind. I was inspired. And I hadn't been this motivated in months.

To help the plan feel like it could become a reality, I decided that every day I would tell one person I was going to quit. My reasoning: The more people I told, the more clients I could potentially get, and the more people I would have to stay accountable to. I did not want to back out of this.

It was exciting, at first—sharing the news and talking about what the future might hold. Aside from my boss, though, there was only one person I was nervous to tell: my dad. The faithful public servant who had been working for the federal government since he was just 17 years old. After all our talks about money and work over the years, I worried that he would worry. I also worried that he would tell me it was a stupid idea or that the plan was somehow flawed. I valued his opinion and wanted his support. It took two weeks, and 14 decision-affirming conversations with other people, for me to get the courage to share the details of my new plan with him. Before I could even get into the numbers, he replied with only three words: "You'll do great!" I should've known by then that my dad also trusted my gut instincts.

With the end in sight, I stopped giving my computer screen the middle finger while cursing out loud and crying. I couldn't control my parents' divorce and my family's future, but I could control this—and it felt good to finally have something to look forward to.

# 11

# *may: finding myself in unusual places*

**months sober:** *28*
**income saved:** *24%*
**confidence I can complete this project:** *100%*

When I hit the 10-month mark of the shopping ban, I was surprised to find I couldn't remember the last time I had thought about buying something I didn't need. None of my usual triggers sparked any kind of reaction. Seeing articles with lists of which books must be read that season were easy to ignore now, when I knew how many still sat unread on my bookshelf at home. Coming across ads on websites for my favorite candles was easy to ignore too, even though I'd run out of candles to burn, which I loved doing while writing. Since I had changed the rules in January to allow me to make my own candles, I hadn't actually bought the supplies to do so. But having the option to make them or live without, I was choosing to temporarily live without. I felt content with what I had, and was confident I could coast to the finish line on that emotion.

It helped that I was scheduled to be on the road for 24 days in May. Compared to every month before, this was extreme, both in the length of time I would be away from home and also the number of trips that made up those 24 days. But each trip served a purpose, even the one I really didn't want to take.

My first flight took me to Toronto for work. After I'd submitted countless pleas, my boss had finally agreed to let me hire someone internally to help with our growing content needs, rather than continue to contract everything out to freelancers. In the weeks before my arrival, I had gone through all the resumes, invited a short list of potential candidates to complete writing and editing assignments, and set up interviews for the week I would be in the office. When everything was said and done, we made someone an offer, it was accepted, and I could not have been more relieved. By the time I returned from all my trips, I would have an extra set of hands and eyes on my side of things, and I needed it now more than ever.

During the nearly three years I had been with the company, I hadn't taken a proper vacation once. I would take two or three days off here and there for conferences, but that was it. I even worked during most of the week I was in New York City in February, because there was simply no one I could pass off my tasks to. Being the first managing editor on the team had been an incredible gift in the early days, when I was able to utilize my strengths and shape the role. But being the only person who could write, edit to match our style guide (which I had also created), use the backend of our blog, and more didn't just make me a linchpin—it meant I could not take an extended period of time off. And I needed a break. Yes, deep down, I knew I was going to leave soon. But I still needed a break now.

From Toronto, I flew back to B.C. and spent a week at home in Victoria. Ben had just returned from university for the summer, and we had yet to talk about the divorce in person. He agreed he had been as surprised as Alli and I were: "I thought we grew up in a house where our parents showed us what a happy marriage looked like." The three of us hiked through wooded trails on a mountain near the house and talked at length about what we thought was next. Ben had never been this open with his feelings before. He was quiet, as many engineers are, yet his time away had obviously helped him grow and mature. Every word out of his mouth filled me with pride, but none more than what he said when I asked if he was upset.

"I'm fine," he replied. "I mean, what's done is done."

What was done was done. There was no going back. There was no denying it, and no amount of begging would ever change it. Ben wasn't angry and he wasn't sad. He had seemingly skipped over most of the stages of grief I had gone through and accepted the news for what it was: the truth. Our new reality. The only thing we could do now was move forward. We all knew it, but Ben was the first to say so.

I had spent months worrying about Alli and Ben, stressing about the future, and wondering how I could help steer us down this new path together. That was part of my job description as the oldest. I had helped take care of "the kids" since they were born. But Ben's answer proved he didn't need me as much as I'd worried he would. He was fine. We were all going to be fine. I never imagined he would be the one to guide us out of this negative loop and point us in the right direction, but that's exactly what he did. He guided me out of the sadness, helped me feel the steady ground beneath my feet again, and pointed me in the direction of our new family.

I spent the rest of my week in Victoria working at all hours. On May 20, I was flying back to New York City with Sarah, another friend I had met through the personal finance blogging community years before. From there, we would begin a 10-day road trip, and I wanted to take all 10 days off from work. In order to do that, I had to fit those extra days into the week before, and accomplish all the work in just five. Somehow, I did it. When we boarded our first flight, my eyes were still tired and bloodshot, but I had done it. It was time for a real vacation.

Sarah and I had been planning this trip since before I found out about my parents' divorce. We knew it wouldn't be cheap, especially because the Canadian dollar was low and the exchange rate would be expensive, so we were always looking for ways to save money. A companion ticket helped us get our two return flights for the price of one, and we scoured websites that sell unsold hotel room inventory at discount prices to save on accommodation. Sarah, who wrote for an established luxury travel website, also got us a few free nights at hotels in exchange for a review. And we used discount codes to save on Amtrak tickets and points to pay for a rental car. By the time we set out, everything was booked and we hadn't paid full price for any of it.

Our first stop was New York City. We met Shannon at a Mexican restaurant near Union Square, then took Sarah for her first walk around the Strand bookstore. Known for containing 18 miles of books, the Strand was my favorite place to go every time I went to the city. I always spent at least an hour walking up and down the aisles, and to this day, after making many more trips there, I don't think I've covered half of the space. I had never actually purchased a book at the Strand, because most of my trips to the city had been during the shopping ban—including this one. It seemed like either a cruel joke or twisted game I kept playing, but I couldn't stop. Even if I couldn't buy something, going to New York City and not visiting the Strand was, for me, like going to Paris and not seeing the Eiffel Tower. I had to go. I had to see it.

From New York, we took the Amtrak to Boston, where we ate pastrami sandwiches at Sam LaGrassa's and cannoli from Mike's Pastry. We took in history lessons along the Freedom Trail and stood heavy with emotion at the New England Holocaust Memorial. We walked down the narrow brick roads of Beacon Hill and past the row houses, through the Boston Common, then along Commonwealth Avenue and down to the waterfront. When we returned to our hotel room that night, we made a pot of black tea, put our tired feet up, and slowly ate the eclairs from Mike's that we'd saved for late-night treats, one bite at a time. If the trip had ended that day, I would have been satisfied.

On our second day, we took the subway over to Cambridge so we could visit Harvard University. I might not have had the opportunity to receive an Ivy League education, but for just one day, I could pretend to imagine what it might feel like. We got ice cream just outside of campus, then found our way over to the Harvard Yard, so we could escape the heat in the shaded grass. Campus workers, students, and tourists rushed around us from all sides. The only creatures that stopped to look at us were the many squirrels of Harvard, who, I imagined, were silently hoping we would hand over the last bites of our sugar cones. When we were done, we willed ourselves to go back out in the sun for a full walk around campus, but not before rubbing the toe of John Harvard's left shoe for good luck.

From Boston, we took the train back to New York City for the weekend and decided we couldn't leave without seeing our first Broadway show. I had now been to the city four times and still had not made my way into a theater. True, musical theater had never been my first choice of entertainment, but this was different. Broadway shows in New York City are special. There is something for everyone. We stood in line at the TKTS discount booth in Times Square and purchased two tickets for *Chicago* that night. When we arrived and received our programs, we were thrilled to see Brandy Norwood—one of our favorite singers when we were kids—was performing as Roxie Hart. Three hours later, we were skipping back to our hotel, waving our hands by our sides, and singing the lyrics to "All That Jazz." We were still singing it when we picked up our rental car the next morning, drove through Times Square, and out of the city.

For the next week, Sarah and I found ourselves in places I had never expected to go. Before we set out, all we had done was booked hotel rooms. We knew where we would be sleeping at night, but we had no plans for how we would spend our days in each city. While driving from New York to Philadelphia, we made a random pit stop and toured parts of Princeton University. *Let's pretend we're getting a second Ivy League education for a couple of hours!* We learned that Philadelphia was home not only to the Liberty Bell, but also to some of the best food either of us had had in the entire country. We also learned that the National Mall in Washington, D.C., wasn't actually a mall but an enormous park, with the Lincoln Memorial on one end and the United States Capitol on the other, surrounded by other memorials, museums, and Smithsonians. And did I mention I drove a car through Times Square and lived to tell the tale?

In both Philadelphia and Washington, D.C., the hotel chain where Sarah had managed to score us free rooms happened to be none other than the Ritz-Carlton. I had never imagined myself as the type of person who would stay in a fancy hotel. The fact that the only word I could find to describe it was "fancy" proved I probably did not belong there. Walking in wearing my $5 T-shirt and khakis from the Gap only further proved how out of place I was. But it was there that I learned luxury hotels do provide an experience you will actually remember. Upon arrival, the valet somehow knew our names, even before we greeted him. In our rooms, we found plates covered in homemade candies with the unique hashtag we had been using on Instagram written in chocolate drizzle: #sarahandcaitgoeast. When we returned to our rooms each night, our beds had been turned down for the evening: Housekeeping had closed the curtains, turned on our bedside lamps, pulled back the covers, and placed a handful of chocolates on our pillows. Sarah was accustomed to turndown service, but I hadn't even known of its existence until this trip.

On one of our last days, we watched a rainbow come up just as the sun started to go down over the Georgetown waterfront, and I realized I was finally starting to feel okay. I wasn't happy every minute of every day. I had shed a few tears on the train from Boston to New York City, and I exchanged a few worried text messages with Alli. But I was okay. On the road with Sarah, I had smiled, joked, laughed, danced, and sung again. I had taken the time off that I needed. Most importantly, I had put myself first. I gave up the feeling that I owed anyone anything, or that I could be someone to everyone. I did what I wanted when I wanted to do it. I put my happiness first. And I was okay. The pictures we took of that moment were beautiful, and have hung framed in my heart ever since.

With every mile we drove and every city we visited, I realized I had the shopping ban to thank for bringing me here—and for allowing me to travel so much this year. Since I was a kid getting ready to graduate from high school, I had proclaimed my desire to see more of the world, but never seemed to have the money to do so. Before this year, the only out-of-country trip I had gone on without my family (that wasn't for work or a conference) was to Las Vegas for a girls' weekend—and that was only possible because of how unbelievably cheap Vegas used to be. My friends would gush over the details of their adventures roaming around Europe and Southeast Asia and Australia and New Zealand, while I said no to trips to Costa Rica, Nicaragua, and the Dominican Republic. My reasoning, at the time, was always that I never had the money. It was true. When I looked at my bank accounts, it was true. But if I had looked around my apartment, instead, I would have seen that I did have money—or at least, I had access to credit. I was simply choosing to spend it on other things.

I had also always claimed I couldn't take time off work, and I certainly couldn't afford to take unpaid time off work. I thought I needed to earn more so I could buy more of what I wanted. And then I wanted even more stuff, which meant I needed to earn even more money. This was a cycle that gave me a lot of stuff, a lot of debt, and not much else. Suddenly it dawned on me that I couldn't remember most of the stuff I'd gotten rid of in the past 11 months, but I could recall details from every one of the trips I had been on. I didn't need to bring souvenirs back with me. I would be able to taste the food and see the sights and remember how the sun felt on my skin in each one forever. This was what I had wanted since I was a teenager, and I finally had it. I was finally starting to live the lifestyle I had always dreamed of.

On the last night of our trip, Sarah and I sat on our beds with our laptops open, banging out freelance articles we owed clients, and scheduling calls and meetings for the week ahead. Sarah had taken the leap and quit her job to work for herself almost a year before, and she was a constant source of inspiration for me. She modeled the definition of what I hoped my own "success" would look like in the future: working during the hours she was most productive, spending more time with the people she loved, and traveling the world. I asked if she thought I would actually be able to work for myself. "Connecting with people is your superpower, Cait," she answered, followed by the same thing my dad had said: "You'll do great!"

During our drive back to New York City, where we would catch our flight home, I received an e-mail with an offer I could not refuse. After telling so many people I had been planning on going out on my own soon, one of my clients wrote to say they had enough work to keep me busy until the end of the year. I could start as soon as I was able to, and work as much or as little as I wanted. "Does that sound like something you'd be interested in?" Truthfully,

I didn't know. It wasn't exactly the type of work I had wanted to jump into, and it didn't pay anywhere near the amount I could earn with some other clients. But I knew what the offer was really presenting: an opportunity to get out—to make my exit. I was still scared to take the leap. I wasn't sure if I was ready, and I didn't know what I would do if this client dropped me—or if any of my other clients dropped me in the future. The only thing I knew for certain was that, thanks to all the extra freelance I'd started doing, I had stockpiled enough cash to make it last until the end of the year. And even if I could only make self-employment work until then, wouldn't it be worth it?

When I got home, I called my boss and gave her a month's notice. By the time the shopping ban was over, I would be free.

# 12

# *june:*
# *packing up*
# *and moving on*

**months sober:** *29*
**income saved:** *42%*
**total number of belongings tossed:** *70%*
**confidence I can complete this project:** *100%*

The final weeks of the shopping ban came with more
uncertainty than I had experienced all year, only this
time I thrived on it. I would wake up in the morning and
feel the adrenaline wash over me, knowing I was one day
closer to being my own boss. It had me walking around
my apartment on the tips of my toes and, occasionally,
I'd catch myself dancing in the kitchen as I waited for my
coffee to brew. I sat a little taller at my desk, while I worked
to cross off every last task from my to-do list. With my

shoulders back, I took deeper breaths that filled my lungs and my body with hope. The end was near and I could finally breathe again.

Up to this point, some of the things I learned to love most about myself had only become evident when I was changing my life. Digging myself out of debt showed me how much determination I had. Living on a tight budget proved I could be more resourceful. Taking control of my health confirmed I was, in fact, in control of my body and my mind-set. Not drinking alcohol continued to teach me I didn't need to be under any influence to have—or be—fun. And giving up shopping for a year demonstrated I had more willpower than I thought, and I was happier when my attention wasn't focused on what I could acquire. Each of those challenges forced me to adjust my habits and push myself outside of my comfort zone. I had different concerns and fears during each one, but many of those stemmed from the same thing: change, and the uncertainty that comes with it. Quitting my job and working for myself would be no different, but I was ready for it.

Still, that doesn't mean I wasn't scared. For every time I caught myself dancing in the kitchen, I also found myself stopping and wondering what I had just given up. Stable work and regular paychecks. I would run the numbers on a handful of different scenarios for how much I might earn each month and see how it would affect my budget and my plans. Then I would look at how much I had saved—only $1,000 less than my original goal—and be reminded that I could make it work. I had given myself five months to save the amount I wanted, and had stashed away the majority of it in only three. Saving for something was easy now that I had a goal. I was determined and I was resourceful and I could make it work.

The thing I was most afraid of had nothing to do with the numbers. It was the act of having to call my boss and quit. She really had taken a chance on me, and I think I will always feel I owe her for that. But she was also my friend and an incredible role model for anyone—not just women—who wanted to someday start their own business. She taught me about the financial side of things, of course. But she also showed me how important it was to work with people I loved and who loved what they did. The way she could switch from talking in a meeting about six-figure deals to asking if you'd seen the latest episode of a reality show proved you should never take yourself too seriously. And our last-minute calls where she would get me to run through talking points before she did a live television interview were just one of the many ways she exemplified how important it was to ask for help. I had never worked with someone like her before. Thinking back to all my previous jobs, it made sense why I had always left them in the same state of apathy. I wasn't challenged and I wasn't learning, and, therefore, I wasn't growing. She showed me it was possible to experience all of those things—to be challenged, to learn, to grow—in one position, and I would experience it again every day after I left. I had been happy for a long time in that role, and never imagined I would quit, especially to go out on my own. Working for myself had never been part of the plan. But now I wondered if it had always been my destiny. If taking a chance on each other, learning from her, and going out on my own after was exactly what was supposed to happen. She confirmed this idea when I told her about my plans. "I always knew I would get this call one day, Cait." I could feel her smile through the phone.

It was a hectic month for us. We started the process of hiring my replacement, but with vacation schedules, they wouldn't make the final decision until weeks after I was gone. In the meantime, I trained a handful of people on the team who I would pass my work off to, created documents outlining my tasks for the new editor, and came up with a process our freelancers could work with in the interim. This was the first time in months it had felt like my organizational skills were being put to good use.

As my end date got closer, I couldn't stop my thoughts from drifting away from work and toward questions about the future. What were my days going to look like? Could I put more energy into my own blog? How would I juggle that on top of freelance work? Would I be okay if a client dropped me? What would I do if all my clients dropped me? Whenever these concerns took me too far down this line of thought, I looked at the numbers and reminded myself I would be okay. I had enough work lined up to survive until the end of the year. I didn't know what would happen after that, but if I could do this for even six months of my life, it would be worth it. Living with so many unknowns wasn't going to be easy, but I had done it before. In fact, I had been doing it ever since I had gotten sober. "Living one day at a time / Enjoying one moment at a time."

My last day at work was June 26, 2015. After getting my in-box down to zero, I peeled off the note that had been taped to my computer since April. July 1 was not only a stretch goal, it had seemed like an impossible feat back in April. I should have known by now that anything was possible if I made it a priority.

At the same time I quit my job, I started thinking about moving back to my hometown. I had originally left Victoria for this job in 2012, and I'd assumed I wouldn't be able to go back until I retired. I had always thought the only way to lead a successful life would be to climb a corporate career ladder, which wasn't really an option in Victoria. It was a government town, and I didn't want to go back to that either. I also didn't want to work at a job where all I cared about was getting a promotion and a raise every year, and when you live in a big city, it can feel like that's all there is to work toward. More work, more money, more stuff. I didn't want any of it. And now, I didn't need any of it. All I needed was to make enough money to live, save, and occasionally travel, and the shopping ban showed me exactly how much that would cost.

The other reason I was so drawn to the idea of moving back was because smaller cities naturally come with slower lifestyles, and are filled with communities of people who are grateful for all the little things life has to offer. I wanted to be surrounded by those who valued living over working, spending time outdoors over spending time online, and doing things for themselves over paying for every possible convenience. I had moved to Toronto and then Greater Vancouver because I thought I needed to be in a big city to build a name and career for myself, but I had never stopped to consider if that was what I actually wanted. It wasn't. I knew what my values were now, and I wanted to live in a city with people who shared them. Plus, if I was going to be working for myself, I could live anywhere. Why wouldn't I want to be in the same city as my family and friends? I didn't know if I would move back forever, but I also knew nothing lasted forever. If I was going to continue living one day at a time, that was where I wanted to do it.

As I started packing and reflected on the past year, I began to laugh at how ludicrous this experiment must have sounded to my loved ones in the beginning. First, I told them I wasn't going to shop for an entire year, which was naturally met with raised eyebrows and questions. But then I added an extra tidbit of information, which was that I also planned to get rid of anything I owned that I didn't use or love. At the time, I couldn't make a well-versed argument for how the two things were connected or why I wanted to do both at the same time. I had simply used that line in my blog post: "I'm still not the mindful consumer I'd like to be." I didn't know what the ultimate goal was, or what I was truly signing myself up for. I simply jumped in with both feet but without a compass, like I usually did, and hoped for the best.

In challenging myself to not shop for an entire year, I was setting myself up either for failure or for the most prosperous year of my life, and I'm happy to say it was the latter. Throughout the entire journey, I was forced to slow down, discover my triggers to spend and to overconsume, and face and change my bad habits. I gave up the things marketers try to convince us we should want in life: the newest and greatest of everything, anything that can fix our problems, and whatever is in style. I exchanged it all for basic necessities and, after a year of not being able to buy anything new, realized that was all I needed. That was all anybody needed. I had always been stuck in the cycle of wanting more, buying more, and then needing more money. The ban uncovered the truth, which was that when you decide to want less, you can buy less and, ultimately, need less money.

Decluttering and purging 70 percent of my belongings came with different lessons. I realized I had spent the first 29 years of my life doing and buying whatever I could to be someone I thought I should be. I kept so many things, and consumed the wrong things, all because I never felt like I was good enough. I wasn't smart enough or professional enough or talented enough or creative enough. I didn't trust that who I was or what I brought to the table in any situation was already unique, so I bought things that could make me better. Then I spent a year sorting through the mess and figuring out who I really was. A writer and a reader. Hiker and traveler. Dog owner and animal lover. Sister, daughter, and friend. It turned out I had never been someone who valued material objects. I valued the people in my life and the experiences we shared together. None of that could be found in the belongings in my home. It had always been in my heart.

If I had simply stopped shopping for a year, I might have learned a lot about myself as a consumer. And if I had simply decluttered my home, I might have learned a lot about my interests. But doing both challenges at the same time was important, because it forced me to stop living on autopilot and start questioning my decisions. Who was I? What was I already good at? What did I care about? What did I really want in this life? Family history showed that if I was lucky, I would get 85 years on this planet. What did I want to do with them? I would always need to pay for things, just like I would always need to eat food and drink water to survive. That was a fact of life. But I was privileged enough to be in a position where I could choose what to spend money on and what to put into my body. This realization not only helped me become a more mindful consumer and save money in the process, it expanded my capacity to care for others and to feel gratitude for the simple things.

Sometimes I still wondered what my life could have looked like if I'd done things differently. If I had taken all my dad's advice when I was younger and been more responsible with my money. It's the same question I've asked about all my consumption tendencies, especially my drinking habits. What could life have looked like if I hadn't fallen into those traps? But then I remember I had to make those mistakes and learn those lessons in order to become the person I am today. That doesn't mean my parents' energy was wasted. If anything, the reason I was able to come to many of these conclusions in my 20s was probably because of everything they'd taught me growing up. When my gut instinct told me I was doing something that was wrong for me, I have to believe that was partially thanks to my parents. Still, I was always going to make some mistakes. It was only after chasing all the things I thought I should have that I realized what I actually wanted.

When I started this challenge, it was about the spending; the money. That's where this story began, and where many of my stories had begun. And the same way sobriety helped me save money every year, the shopping ban had, in fact, done the same. But looking back, it was never really about the money. The best gift the ban had given me was the tools to take control of my life and get a fresh start as my real self. It challenged me. It turned my life upside down. It helped me save $17,000 in a single year. And then it saved *me*.

As I continued packing, I saw my reflection in the standing mirror in my dining room, and realized I wasn't wearing any makeup. Before the ban, I wouldn't have dared to step out into the world without the basics on my face: eyeliner, eye shadow, and mascara. The thought of people seeing how tired I looked without it was scary. Now I couldn't remember the last time I had put anything on my face except for moisturizer. That was never part of the plan either. I had no opinion on whether or not women should wear makeup, any more than I cared what people spent their money on. It was a personal decision, and I didn't plan on becoming someone who would forgo it. But something I had learned time and time again was that every small change you make pays compound interest. It helps you make another change, another mind-set shift, another decision to live a new way. If I put makeup on again in the future, it wouldn't be to stop people from seeing the real me—it would simply be *for* me.

It only took a few hours to finish packing, now that I owned just 30 percent of the stuff that had once been in my home. Aside from my furniture, my belongings fit into eight small boxes, and my entire wardrobe—now just 29 pieces total—squeezed into a single suitcase. I was happy to carry it out from one home and into another this time, because I knew exactly what was inside of each box. After everything else had been bagged up and donated, all that remained was the real me. It wasn't much, but it was enough.

It was enough. I had enough.

I was enough.

# epilogue

My shopping ban ended on July 6, 2015. Throughout the year, I lived on an average of 51 percent of my income ($28,000), saved 31 percent ($17,000), and spent the other 18 percent on travel ($10,000). I proved that I could live on less, save more, and do more of what I loved, and learned so many other lessons throughout the process. I could have walked away feeling like it was a success. It *was* a success. Instead, I published a post on my blog the next day (my 30th birthday) announcing I was going to carry on and do it for another year.

The rules were essentially the same, except this time I wanted to do something I'd regretted not doing during the first year: tracking every single item I purchased and consumed. The thought of writing down how many tubes of toothpaste I used didn't exactly spark joy, as Marie Kondo would say, but I wanted to add some data points to my research and show readers what an average female consumer might actually need to purchase in a year. I didn't know what to expect, but assumed I would use a lot less than I thought, and I was right. As an example, I went through five sticks of deodorant, four tubes of toothpaste, two bottles of shampoo and two of conditioner. Knowing this about myself isn't necessarily earth-shattering, but it does prevent me from ever thinking I should stockpile toiletries again.

The other reason I wanted to continue the ban was because I hadn't taken advantage of the newer rules I had written for myself in January. I never ran out of cleaning supplies or laundry detergent, so there had been no reason to make either. I also hadn't bothered to make candles or plant a garden yet, and instead opted to live without. But moving back to Victoria confirmed I did want to take on these challenges. I planted a small garden and learned I don't have a green thumb, but I'm glad I carried on and tried anyway. Some people are just meant to take care of succulents and cacti.

On the decluttering front, I continue to bag up and donate things I don't use, and I have gotten rid of somewhere between 75 and 80 percent of my belongings. The most frequently asked question I get about that is if there's anything I regret letting go of, and the answer is no. Truthfully, I don't even remember what most of it was. One item I do remember selling in the second year of the ban was a brand-name purse that I always felt embarrassed to have on my shoulder. If you met me, you'd see a girl who wears the same black leggings and flannel shirts almost every single day. I am not a brand-name kind of person, but I held on to that purse for years because it seemed like something professional Cait should have. When the second yearlong shopping ban was over, I traded it in for a 60-liter backpack I can take with me on overnight hiking trips. That is something I will never be embarrassed to own.

Travel continues to be the one thing I value spending money on. In the second year of the ban, I traveled to Portland, Oregon; Charlotte, North Carolina; Toronto, Winnipeg, Salt Spring Island, Galiano Island, Tofino, and Vancouver; and numerous times to Squamish (where I would eventually move). And when it was over, I went on a seven-week road trip around the United States by myself. While I have the freedom and money to do something "bigger," like live and work from a foreign country for a few months, I've realized I care more about exploring North America first. It's far too easy to take your surroundings for granted, and I am blessed to live in one of the most beautiful parts of this continent.

When the second year was over, I decided not to repeat the experiment, but only because it had become a way of life. I don't keep an inventory (truthfully, I never did after I first created it), but I do only buy things when I need them, and never simply because they are on sale. You might think that means I spend more when I shop; however, the opposite is still true because I don't waste money on anything. Every purchase I make is carefully considered, not done on impulse. I haven't made a blackout purchase since Black Friday in 2014 (and have barely used my old e-reader since then either). I do buy books on occasion now, but only if I know I'm going to read them right away, and I usually pass them on to a friend or to my local library when I'm done.

My family is doing fine. We're still figuring out what this new normal looks like, but we're doing it together, which I should have always trusted would be the case. I'm sad to share that "the girls"—our beloved dogs—both passed away in May 2017, but lived their final years in our family home and were loved until the very end.

As for work, I'm still my own boss, and continually have to remind myself that I have no way of predicting what the future holds—and that's okay. I don't know what's next for me. I don't know what work I'll do, how much I'll earn, or where I'll travel to next. I didn't even know I would get the opportunity to write this book until it happened. All I know is that I'm content with life as it is. I also have five years of sobriety behind me now, and I'm confident I'll never drink again, no matter what life throws at me.

Today I consider myself a former binge consumer turned mindful consumer of everything. I continue to experiment with consuming less of things I feel I'm not getting any value from, including doing a 30-day social media detox and another month without television. Whether it's these experiments or the shopping ban, I still hear some people's concerns about how a ban feels too restrictive. While I understand how easy this is to worry about, my advice is always the same: Remember that all you're committing to is slowing down and asking yourself what you really want, rather than acting on impulse. That's it. That's what being a "mindful" consumer is all about.

One of the greatest lessons I learned during these years is that whenever you're thinking of binging, it's usually because some part of you or your life feels like it's lacking—and nothing you drink, eat, or buy can fix it. I know, because I've tried it all and none of it worked. Instead, you have to simplify, strip things away, and figure out what's really going on. Falling into the cycle of wanting more, consuming more, and needing even more won't help.

More was never the answer. The answer, it turned out, was always less.

# *your*
# *guide*
# *to less*

Hi friend,

If reading my story has inspired you to do a similar experiment of your own, let me first say: I am so excited for you! A challenge like this isn't easy, but I know it's possible to get to the end feeling like you've changed your spending habits and figured out what you value most in life.

In saying that, I also know that wanting to start a challenge like this and successfully completing it are two different things. There are what-if situations to prepare for, personal goals and rules to set, and even other people to consider. During the experience, you may realize things about yourself that were always present but hid securely behind your spending power. And if you do it for long enough, my guess is you'll become more resourceful than you knew you could be.

I want you to get to that point. I don't want any of the what-if situations to hold you back or cause you to relapse or even give up on your experiment altogether. I want you to push through each and every one, so you can discover more about yourself and find creative ways to get through this world without opening your wallet. Your financial goals might be to spend less, save more money in general, save for something specific, or simply become a more mindful consumer. My goal with this guide is to help you get organized and push through to the end, so you can reach your goal—whatever it may be.

Before you get started, I would encourage you to spend some time thinking about one thing: the reason you want to take on a challenge such as this in the first place. Some people call this their "why." It might be the same reason you do anything in life, or it could be very specific to this challenge. If you need help determining your why, consider where you're at in your life's journey so far and ask yourself these questions. What do you want right now? What do you want to get out of this life? What mark do you want to leave on the world? And why?

Throughout the challenge, I would also encourage you to keep a list of your values. Your values should not be your aspirations—confusing the two is just one of the reasons I used to buy things for the ideal version of myself. Instead, your values can be defined as both your principles or standards of behavior, and as your judgment of what is important in life. Whenever you realize what one of your values is, add it to the list. Keep this nearby (perhaps even in your wallet).

By the time you finish your own experiment, my hope is you will be living a lifestyle that aligns with your goals and values—and that your budget aligns with them too. When everything is working together, it's a lot easier to find inner peace, appreciation, and gratitude for all you have.

Good luck!

## 1. Declutter Your Home

Before you begin a shopping ban for any length of time, I would suggest going through your home and getting rid of anything that doesn't serve a purpose in your life. Don't just organize your stuff—analyze it, ask yourself what you want to keep, and let go of all the rest. I'm sure that sounds counterintuitive to some degree. You're not going to be allowed to shop for three months, six months, or a year, and you're also going to get rid of the things you currently have? But decluttering first can open your eyes to how much stuff you've wasted money on in the past, which can serve as motivation to not waste more money during your shopping ban. It will also give you a visual reminder of how much stuff you're keeping.

## 2. Take Inventory

It's easy to forget how much stuff you own when it lives inside closets, drawers, and boxes. While you're decluttering, I suggest also taking inventory of the items you own the most of. You don't have to be as exact as I was, where I literally wrote down things like how many pens I owned. Instead, try this: Go through each room of your home and write down the top five items you have the most of. For example, in your bathroom, you might have a lot of shampoo, conditioner, lotion, toothpaste, and deodorant. Take inventory of those items and write down the number you currently have "in stock." These are some of the things you will not be allowed to buy during your shopping ban—at least, not until you run out of them and need more.

### 3. Write Three Lists

When you were decluttering and taking inventory, two things probably started to become clear: There are things in your home you definitely don't need to buy more of, and there are probably also a few things you will, in fact, need to buy during your shopping ban. At this point, it's time to write three lists.

- **The Essentials List:\*** This is a list of things you're allowed to buy whenever you run out of them. The easiest way to create this list is to walk around your home and look at what you use in each room every day. For me, this included things like groceries and toiletries. I also included gifts for others.

- **The Nonessentials List:\*** This is a list of things you're not allowed to buy during your shopping ban. For me, that included things I thought I would enjoy but didn't use on a daily basis, like books, magazines, and candles. If you took inventory of any of these items, add the number you have beside it for reference.

- **The Approved Shopping List:** This is a list of specific things you're allowed to buy during your shopping ban. As you declutter and take stock of what you own, think about what's coming up during the time span of your shopping ban and figure out what you might need to add to this list.

\*You'll notice I didn't include any "experience" costs, like dining out or going on a vacation. If you want to include that stuff in either list, you can! But you don't have to. I added take-out coffee to my nonessentials list, simply because I wasn't comfortable spending a lot of money on it anymore. However, I still allowed myself to go to restaurants occasionally. Remember, your ban should be unique to you.

## 4. Unsubscribe from All Store/Coupon Newsletters

Now that you have your three lists of all the things you are and are not allowed to buy, it's time to remove as many temptations as possible—starting with what gets delivered to your in-box. Whenever a newsletter comes in from a store or service that wants your money, hit unsubscribe. If you want to take this one step further, I suggest unfollowing all your favorite stores on social media. And if you want to take this one extra step further, I suggest also deleting all the bookmarks you have saved of things you wanted to buy "one day." Out of sight, out of mind, my friend.

## 5. Set Up a Shopping Ban Savings Account

No matter what your ultimate goal is, you are going to save money by not shopping. What you do with that money is up to you, but I suggest opening a new savings account (or renaming an existing one you don't use) and making it your dedicated Shopping Ban Savings Account. How much money you decide to put in it each month is up to you. I started by depositing $100 per month, because I knew I was saving that by not buying take-out coffee anymore. Another idea is to transfer over any money you stop yourself from spending by not giving in to an impulse purchase. Finally, you could also deposit any money you make by selling things you decluttered.

If you want an extra reminder to not spend money, put a sticky note around each of the debit and credit cards in your wallet with a reminder that you're on a shopping ban. Write something on it like: "Do you really need it?" or "Is it on your shopping list?"


## 6. Tell Everyone You Know

Start by telling your family, partner, and/or kids— especially anyone who lives in the same household as you and who is part of your family budget. Based on those conversations, you'll need to decide together whether it's something you want everyone to participate in or whether you're going to start with leading by example and doing it alone. There might be some resistance from others, if you want everyone to get on board, so don't push the idea. The most important thing, for now, is to make sure they know about your intentions to not shop for anything besides the essentials for a period of time. Explain what your goals are, how you think it can help you and your family, and even set some goals for what you'll do with all the money you save.

After that, tell the people you spend the most time with. The more people you tell, the more likely it is that you'll stick to your shopping ban, because you'll feel the need to stay accountable to not only yourself but also to them. And I would suggest you have at least one accountability partner who you can call/text whenever you get the urge to shop, so they can stop you.

## 7. Replace Costly Habits with Free/Cheap Alternatives

One of the top concerns people who are considering doing shopping bans share with me is not knowing what they can replace their costly habits with—especially when it involves other people. Telling people "I can't go shopping" or "I can't go out for dinner and drinks" (if you're cutting back on restaurant spending as part of your ban) isn't always a fun conversation to have. However, if you're willing to suggest other free/cheap activities, I think you'll be surprised by how many people are more than happy to do something that will also save them a few dollars. For example, instead of walking around a shopping mall or driving to the outlets, go hiking or explore parts of your neighborhood on foot. And instead of going out for dinner and drinks, suggest hosting barbecues or taking turns hosting potlucks where everyone brings something.

## 8. Pay Attention to Your Triggers (and Change Your Reactions)

Here's where mindfulness comes into play. When you feel the urge to shop, sometimes texting a friend and asking them to stop you isn't enough. You need to pause and consider everything that's happening in your current environment. How do you feel? Did you have a bad day? Where are you (and what brought you there)? Who are you with? And what justifications are you telling yourself? Any/all of these things can be part of the trigger that urges you to buy something, and spotting them is extremely important so you can ultimately change your reactions. If you don't replace bad habits with good habits, you're more likely to "relapse" and go back to your old ways. When something triggers you, figure out what else you can do—besides spending money—and do it repeatedly, until it eventually becomes second nature.

## 9. Learn to Live Without/Become More Resourceful

If you're doing a shopping ban for more than three months, there may be a few times when you'll want to give up, and the only way to push through them is to live without an item for a while. Unless you really need something, try to live without it for at least 30 days, and see how many times you actually miss it. If it becomes a daily annoyance, go ahead and replace it. Otherwise, let it go. Also, depending on what the item is that you're currently living without, finding other ways to fix or source it may be easier than you think. If you can't fix it yourself, borrow it from someone you know or even rent it. The more we share, the less that goes into the landfill.

## 10. Appreciate What You Have

Finally, as time goes on, you'll start to feel grateful for everything that is currently in your life. From the clothes in your closet to the appliances in your kitchen, using what you keep will serve as a reminder that money has already bought you everything you need. Your relationships, and the happiness and health of family and friends, will take top priority. And a walk outside can go a long way to brighten your day. One important thing I've realized is that the success of your shopping ban will depend on the stories you tell yourself. If you think, *This sucks,* then you'll probably end up going on a binge. But if you say, "This item is great but I don't need it," and choose to appreciate what you already have, my guess is you'll never go back for the items you pass up on.

## When You Really Need to Buy Something

Now, even after writing an entire book about not shopping for a year, I do know there will come a time during your shopping ban when you will need something that's not on your approved shopping list. When you find yourself in this situation, ask yourself questions like the ones in the flow chart on page 180.

Note: You don't always need to buy quality pieces. For example, if your kids are young and need new clothes, go for secondhand/free whenever possible, since they'll grow out of them quickly. But if you're replacing something for yourself that you use often, don't always opt for what's cheap. I've made the mistake of buying fast fashion items because they were cheap too many times, and they almost always needed to be replaced again within a few months.

At the end of the day, remember this: The success of your shopping ban will depend on the stories you tell yourself throughout it. If you think it's hard, you run a higher risk of quitting and even binge-shopping after. But if you appreciate what you have and actually use what you buy, the results could be life-changing. My shopping ban coupled with my massive declutter/purge of stuff taught me what I value most in life, and none of it can be bought from a store. I hope you finish your own shopping ban with the same understanding and revelations.

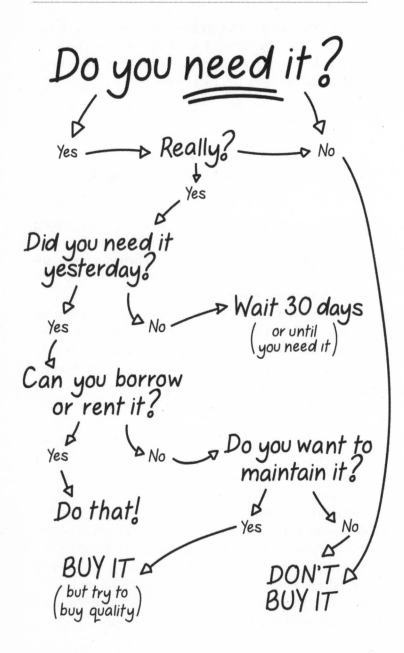

# resources

Throughout this book, I've mentioned a few resources that helped me become more mindful during my year of less. Here is a list of those resources, plus more I've grown to love. I hope they will help you during your own experiment.

## Podcasts

- Hurry Slowly: http://hurryslowly.co/
- Optimal Living Daily: http://oldpodcast.com/
- The Slow Home Podcast: http://slowyourhome.com/the-slow-home-podcast/

## TEDx Talks

- "All It Takes Is 10 Mindful Minutes" with Andy Puddicombe: ted.com/talks/andy_puddicombe_all_it_takes_is_10_mindful_minutes
- "Listening to Shame" with Brené Brown: ted.com/talks/brene_brown_listening_to_shame

## Meditation Apps

- Calm: calm.com
- Headspace: headspace.com
- Insight Timer: insighttimer.com

## Other Apps

- Moment: inthemoment.io

# community

Even when we think we have all the resources and tools in our toolbox, there is often no greater help than the support from our community. I know that one of the reasons I was successful in both getting out of debt and completing my shopping ban experiment is that I had people rooting for me online. Not only did my community give me something to stay accountable to, I knew I could call on them whenever I needed a push or some words of encouragement. I want the same thing to exist for you.

For everyone who takes on a similar challenge in the future, I have created an online community where we can share our stories, our wins, and our struggles. It's a safe space for us to talk about our experiences, offer suggestions, and cheer each other on. And there will be celebrations. Oh, will there be celebrations!

Join the community and share your story at:
caitflanders.com/community

One thing I've always said on my blog is that the more we share, the more we'll all know—and the better off we'll all be. My hope is that this book and our community will inspire thousands of more mindful decisions to be made in the future. But it all starts with you answering one question: What do *you* really want?

xo Cait

# reading group guide

*The Year of Less* charts Cait Flanders's journey through a year-long shopping ban, with the challenges she faced and the surprising discoveries she made along the way. You can use these questions as starting points to discuss Cait's "year of less" and explore your own experience.

- In the beginning of the book, Cait shares that her family always talked about money while she was growing up, and the impact that had on her. What conversations did your family have about money, if any, and how did that impact you? What conversations would you like to have with family or friends in the future?

- Describe a time in your life when you bought something and were disappointed by it. Why did you buy it? And why were you disappointed? Could you have done anything different when making the decision to purchase?

- In chapter 5, Cait shares the dialogue she had with her inner voice, which talked her into breaking the shopping ban and buying something that wasn't on the approved shopping list. Did any part of that resonate with you? What are some of the things your inner voice says to you when you're considering making purchases?

- Cait shares honestly about how most of her self-worth came from being "good" at partying, which made it more difficult for her to understand her self-worth after she quit drinking. Not knowing who she was resulted in her making a lot of misguided purchases. How do you measure your self-worth, and how do you think it impacts your spending?

- Why do you think we encourage one another to spend money, when we all want to be saving or putting more towards the things we really value and want out of life?

- "Whenever you let go of something negative in your life, you make room for something positive." Describe a time in your life when this was true for you.

- If money wasn't a huge stress in your life, what would you want to do with your time? What's stopping you from working toward that? Are there any stories you're telling yourself currently that you can rewrite?

- What stops you from making big life changes or attempting challenges similar to Cait's or others you've heard of? Would giving yourself the freedom to not do it perfectly help you start? And is there anyone or anything that could support you?

- What does the term "mindful consumer" mean to you? What are some ways you want to try to become a more mindful consumer?

# acknowledgments

Since you all now know how much I enjoy lining things up in order, I trust you won't judge me for attempting to do the same with these acknowledgments! I'll start with how this book came together.

First, I have to thank Laura for sharing my story on *Forbes*, and the handful of literary agents who read that story and felt a book was next. I was completely overwhelmed and had no idea how to move forward, but it was those conversations that ultimately led me here.

I will forever be grateful to my friend Chris for introducing me to his agent, who would eventually become mine. Lucinda, this book wouldn't be what it is, without your help. Thank you for being a champion for its success, and for always being honest and keeping it real with me.

I can't imagine the personal stories in this book being shared by any publisher other than the Hay House family— because it *is* a family and I'm grateful they adopted me into it. Patty, hearing you say I could write it exactly how I'd outlined in my proposal was a true *gift*. And Anne, while I'm sure it's obvious I wasn't an English major, you have always made me feel like a good writer. Thank you for honoring my style and helping me pour even more of myself onto these pages.

I'm a firm believer that you can't "do it all"—at least, not alone or all at the same time. Taking time to write this book meant having to take a (temporary) step back from two other projects. I couldn't have done that without my business partners, Carrie and Jay. Thank you for being flexible and supporting me through every step of this journey. I'm so honored to work with you both, and I hope I am at least half the partner to you that you have both been to me.

When my editor first asked me if I wanted to write acknowledgments, I honestly wasn't sure what more I could say. This book is a love letter to my family, and to all the friends who helped me during this year of less. But there are a few people I want to give special mentions to.

Julie, my sounding board in life and in work. We've written thousands of words about our friendship, but now I think I can sum it up in one sentence: you are the person I can be my true self with. Thank you for all the breakfast, coffee, and milkshake breaks.

Pascal, my outdoor adventure partner in crime. Thank you for inspiring me to spend more time outside; that is where I feel like my best self and I'm grateful I get to share it with you. I can't wait to see what Adventure Tuesday looks like when we are old and gray.

Alyssa, thank you for holding space for my pain and helping me feel less alone. I know Toby, Molly, and Lexie are keeping each other company now too.

I also have to thank Shannon for inspiring me to be a better writer, Amanda for celebrating every milestone of this book with me, and Marci for being the first person to think I could write one.

I know I wouldn't be here without all my friends in the blogging community, as well as the amazing people who read mine. I have never been able to find the exact right words to describe my understanding and appreciation of that, so I will just say this: I am grateful for you.

Finally, even though this book was a love letter to them already, I have to thank my family for always believing in me. Thank you for fostering my love of reading and encouraging me to write. Thank you for throwing book ideas at me and imagining I would be an author one day. I didn't know this would ever be possible, but you guys did. We are so fortunate to have a family as close as ours. I would be lost without us.

And that includes you too, Emma. You are my family, and I love you.

# ABOUT THE AUTHOR

 **Cait Flanders** is a former binge consumer turned mindful consumer of everything. Through personal stories, she writes about what happens when money, minimalism and mindfulness cross paths. Cait's story has been shared in *The New York Times*, *The Guardian*, *The Globe and Mail*, *Vogue*, Oprah.com, Forbes.com and more. She inspires people to consume less and live more. Cait is from Victoria, B.C., Canada, but spends most of her time exploring the world.

**www.caitflanders.com**

notes

# notes

notes

# notes

# notes

# notes

## Hay House Titles of Related Interest

*YOU CAN HEAL YOUR LIFE, the movie,*
starring Louise Hay & Friends
(available as a 1-DVD program, an expanded
2-DVD set, and an online streaming video)
Learn more at www.hayhouse.com/louise-movie

*THE SHIFT, the movie,*
starring Dr. Wayne W. Dyer
(available as a 1-DVD program, an expanded
2-DVD set, and an online streaming video)
Learn more at www.hayhouse.com/the-shift-movie

*BLOOM: A Tale of Courage, Surrender, and
Breaking through Upper Limits,* by Bronnie Ware

*LET IT OUT: A Journey through Journaling,*
by Katie Dalebout

*WHAT YOUR CLUTTER IS TRYING TO
TELL YOU: Uncover the Message in the Mess and
Reclaim Your Life,* by Kerri L. Richardson

*YOU ARE AMAZING: A Help-Yourself Guide to
Trusting Your Vibes + Reclaiming Your Magic,*
by Sonia and Sabrina Choquette-Tully

All of the above are available at www.hayhouse.co.uk

# Hay House Podcasts
*Bring Fresh, Free Inspiration Each Week!*

Hay House proudly offers a selection of life-changing audio content via our most popular podcasts!

### Hay House Meditations Podcast

Features your favorite Hay House authors guiding you through meditations designed to help you relax and rejuvenate. Take their words into your soul and cruise through the week!

### Dr. Wayne W. Dyer Podcast

Discover the timeless wisdom of Dr. Wayne W. Dyer, world-renowned spiritual teacher and affectionately known as "the father of motivation." Each week brings some of the best selections from the 10-year span of Dr. Dyer's talk show on HayHouseRadio.com.

### Hay House World Summit Podcast

Over 1 million people from 217 countries and territories participate in the massive online event known as the Hay House World Summit. This podcast offers weekly mini-lessons from World Summits past as a taste of what you can hear during the annual event, which occurs each May.

### Hay House Radio Podcast

Listen to some of the best moments from HayHouseRadio.com, featuring expert authors such as Dr. Christiane Northrup, Anthony William, Caroline Myss, James Van Praagh, and Doreen Virtue discussing topics such as health, self-healing, motivation, spirituality, positive psychology, and personal development.

### Hay House Live Podcast

Enjoy a selection of insightful and inspiring lectures from Hay House Live, an exciting event series that features Hay House authors and leading experts in the fields of alternative health, nutrition, intuitive medicine, success, and more! Feel the electricity of our authors engaging with a live audience, and get motivated to live your best life possible!

*Find Hay House podcasts on iTunes, or visit www.HayHouse.com/podcasts for more info.*

# HAY HOUSE

*Look within*

Join the conversation about latest products,
events, exclusive offers and more.

**f**  Hay House UK

🐦  @HayHouseUK

📷  @hayhouseuk

❤  healyourlife.com

*We'd love to hear from you!*